THE VIETNAM WARS

50 YEARS AGO— TWO COUNTRIES TORN APART

LIFE BOOKS

Managing Editor
Robert Sullivan
Director of Photography
Barbara Baker Burrows
Creative Direction
Li'l Robin Design, Inc.
Deputy Picture Editor
Christina Lieberman
Copy Chief
Barbara Gogan
Copy Editor
Parlan McGaw
Writer-Reporters
Elizabeth L. Bland, Mary Hart,
Daniel S. Levy, Amy Lennard
Goehner
Associate Photo Editor
Sarah Cates
Editorial Assistant
Courtney Mifsud
Photo Assistant
Caitlin Powers
Consulting Picture Editors
Mimi Murphy (Rome),
Tala Skari (Paris) Tala Skari

Special Contributing Editor
Andrea Barbalich

Special thanks: Benjamin Buckley;
Kelly Crager, Vietnam Center and
Archive, Texas Tech University;
Lieutenant Colonel Donald Wright;
Amy Wong

"America's Timeline" source:
20th Century Day by Day

TIME INC. PREMEDIA

Richard K. Prue (Director), Richard
Shaffer (Production), Keith Aurelio,
Jen Brown, Neal Clayton, Charlotte
Coco, Liz Grover, Kevin Hart, Mert
Kerimoglu, Rosalie Khan, Patricia
Koh, Marco Lau, Brian Mai, Po
Fung Ng, Rudi Papiri, Barry Pribula,
Clara Renauro, Vaune Trachtman

TIME HOME ENTERTAINMENT
Publisher
Jim Childs
Vice President and Associate Publisher
Margot Schupf
Vice President, Finance
Vandana Patel
Executive Director, Marketing Services
Carol Pittard
**Executive Director, Business
Development** Suzanne Albert
Executive Director, Marketing
Susan Hettleman
Publishing Director
Megan Pearlman
Associate Director of Publicity
Courtney Greenhalgh
Assistant General Counsel
Simone Procas
Assistant Director, Special Sales
Ilene Schreider
**Senior Marketing Manager, Sales
Marketing** Danielle Costa
Senior Book Production Manager
Susan Chodakiewicz
Senior Manager, Category Marketing
Bryan Christian

Marketing Manager
Isata Yansaneh
Associate Prepress Manager
Alex Voznesenskiy
Associate Project Manager
Stephanie Braga

Editorial Director
Stephen Koepp
Senior Editor
Roe D'Angelo
Copy Chief
Rina Bander
Design Manager
Anne-Michelle Gallero
Assistant Managing Editor
Gina Scauzillo

Special thanks: Katherine Barnet,
Brad Beatson, Jeremy Biloon,
Rose Cirrincione, Assu Etsubneh,
Mariana Evans, Christine Font,
Hillary Hirsch, David Kahn, Jean
Kennedy, Amy Mangus, Kimberly
Marshall, Nina Mistry, Dave
Rozzelle, Matthew Ryan, Ricardo
Santiago, Divyam Shrivastava,
Adriana Tierno

Copyright © 2014 Time Home
Entertainment Inc.

Published by LIFE BOOKS,
an imprint of Time Home
Entertainment Inc.
1271 Avenue of the Americas, 6th Fl.
New York, New York 10020

ISBN 10: 1-61893-101-6
ISBN 13: 978-1-61893-101-6
Library of Congress Control
Number: 2014932048

"LIFE" is a registered trademark of
Time Inc.

We welcome your comments and
suggestions about LIFE Books.
Please write to us at:
LIFE Books
Attention: Book Editors
PO Box 11016
Des Moines, IA 50336-1016

If you would like to order any of
our hardcover Collector's Edition
books, please call us at 1-800-
327-6388 (Monday through
Friday, 7 a.m.–8 p.m., or Saturday,
7 a.m.–6 p.m., Central Time).

ENDPAPERS Front: Legendary
combat photographer Horst Faas
captures U.S. Army helicopters
during an attack on a Vietcong
camp in March 1965. *Photograph
by Horst Faas/AP.* **Back:** Half
a million people protest the
Vietnam War in Washington, D.C.,
on November 15, 1969.
*Photograph by Barton Silverman/
The New York Times/Redux*

PAGE 1 Larry Burrows spent nine
years covering the Vietnam War.
Among the many works of his
included in this book is this shot
of U.S. Army Captain Robert
Bacon taken in 1964. *Photograph
by Larry Burrows © Larry
Burrows Collection*

PAGES 2–3 In a never-before-
published photograph, Judy
Collins performs at the March
on Washington to End the War
in Vietnam on April 17, 1965.
Photograph © Daniel Kramer

THESE PAGES Burrows, famous
for finding ways to capture the
impossible, would affix cameras
to military aircraft and sometimes
have the doors of planes removed
so he could lean out and shoot as
if he were outside the plane. Here,
his photograph of AC-47 tracer fire
pinpointing a jungle target in 1966.
Photograph by Larry Burrows/LIFE

THE VIETNAM WARS

50 YEARS AGO— TWO COUNTRIES TORN APART

EVERYONE AT WAR

The title of our book—*The Vietnam Wars,* with an *s*—might be seen as provocative, but it is not intended that way. Our point is: There were two battlefronts for America as the 1960s wore on—on the far side of the world and here at home. While Washington ramped up its efforts against the communist North Vietnamese, protests in the streets and on the nation's campuses escalated apace. Also, there had been an earlier war against the Vietminh, too little understood by Americans, in which, during and then immediately after World War II, France tried to maintain possession of its Indochinese colonies: Vietnam, Laos and Cambodia. The United States sent "advisers" to assist the French beginning as far back as 1950, and thus entered Vietnam. A half century ago in 1965, more than a decade after the French had been defeated by Ho Chi Minh, President Lyndon Baines Johnson authorized the deployment of the first official United States ground troops—3,500 Marines. Escalation was swift; progress was not. America would eventually be engaged in Vietnam for more than two decades, with horrific consequences.

What do we remember of the Vietnam wars? Reminders are in the pages that follow: an exotic, beautiful land of rice paddies and forests serving as a hellish theater of war; westerners bringing their western ways to an eastern land they didn't understand; terrible instances when innocent children were caught in the crossfire; fallen protesters at Kent State and the violence in Chicago; a White House besieged; bravery and comradeship in the field; napalm fire; confusion—constant confusion.

American journalists and photojournalists, including LIFE's,

covered all of the many different conflicts, and with this book we look at the various fights with the benefit of historical context. Henry Luce, who founded LIFE in 1936, said that he did not "plan LIFE as a war magazine [but] it turned out that way." Indeed, pictures from the front lines during World War II—Robert Capa went in with the first wave on D-Day—stunned our readers. The tradition continued during the Korean War, distinguished by the work of David Douglas Duncan among others. Now came this other business in Indochina. Duncan was well familiar with the scene—his 1953 photo-essay on the region, "Indochina, All But Lost" was revelatory—and later his pictures of the fighting at Con Thien, one of which is seen on the cover of our book, were as dramatic as they were terribly beautiful. Also arriving in Vietnam early was LIFE staffer John Dominis, and his work is in these pages. So is that of Larry Burrows, who would be associated with this war as Duncan had been with Korea;

of Carl Mydans, who had spent part of World War II in a Japanese prison camp and was now back in a war zone; of Capa again (he would be killed stepping on a landmine in Thai Binh, Vietnam, while shooting for LIFE in 1954); of Paul Schutzer (who would be killed shooting for LIFE on the first day of Israel's Six Day War in 1967); of Co Rentmeester, John Olson, Howard Sochurek and Joe Scherschel.

"We happy few," Burrows said of the photojournalists who covered war, quoting Shakespeare's Henry V, "we band of brothers." In Vietnam, he was preeminent among them. London-born, Burrows was a tall, bespectacled man whose sense of compassion imbued his work. He was 44 in 1971 when he too was killed, the helicopter in

Photo credits (vertical, left to right): JOHN OLSON/THE LIFE IMAGES COLLECTION/GETTY · ALFRED EISENSTAEDT/LIFE · JOHN OLSON/LIFE · PAUL SCHUTZER/LIFE

LARRY BURROWS is wearing the glasses on the opposite page; the Associated Press photographer Horst Faas is with him in Saigon in 1964. Above, clockwise from top left: David Douglas Duncan in Khe Sanh in 1968; John Olson in an unidentified Vietnamese village in 1968; Carl Mydans in the Mekong Delta during the Tet Offensive of 1968; Paul Schutzer (left) and LIFE associate editor Michael Mok in Vietnam in 1965; Co Rentmeester having been wounded in 1968.

which he was traveling with fellow photographers Henri Huet, Kent Potter and Keisaburo Shimamato shot down over Laos.

Of course there were printside journalists in Vietnam at the time as well, and one of them was a young Bob Schieffer. As he will tell you on the pages immediately following, he was seeking stories about

Texan kids fighting at or near the front. Schieffer admits he went to Vietnam hoping the U.S. would win but remembers how quickly after arriving he realized this outcome was beyond problematic.

In our book, LIFE has asked others to look back. We have talked with a university professor who was involved in the war from start to finish and with the woman who, while still a college student, designed the Vietnam Veterans Memorial. In our final chapter, "Remembering," Joe McNally, who was the last in the storied line of LIFE staff photographers, and writer-reporter Daniel S. Levy went coast-to-coast, assembling a portfolio of thoughts and images— veterans, activists, dissidents all represented. They once fought the Vietnam wars. They remain to tell the tale.

FINDING VIETNAM

BY BOB SCHIEFFER

The thing about Vietnam was always the ironies. In those days, America was the most powerful nation in the world, economically and militarily.

However, for nearly 11 years no initiative—from the grandest nuclear arms negotiations to the smallest domestic program—could be undertaken until we asked the question, "How will this affect the war in Vietnam?"

We had gone to a tiny country that many Americans could not have found on a map. Yet, as opposition to the war grew, it was our own institutions that were threatened and our country that was in danger of being torn apart.

I went to Vietnam in the winter of 1965 as a 27-year-old reporter for my hometown Texas newspaper, the *Fort Worth Star-Telegram.* Until 1965, the American soldiers in Vietnam were "advisers," but

Lyndon Johnson had decided that spring to send in ground combat forces to fight the communists. By December, when I left for Saigon, thousands more were on the way.

Two years earlier, then Defense Secretary Robert McNamara had said the war was going so well he expected all American forces to be brought home by the end of 1965—again ironically, the very period that Lyndon Johnson was beginning the buildup of American forces that would grow to 400,000 by the next year.

McNamara's rosy prediction of 1963 would be among the first of many government pronouncements that proved wrong.

My tour as a foreign correspondent did not get off to a great start. I arrived by commercial airliner at an airport in the Saigon suburbs, wearing a wool suit and lugging an 80-pound suitcase (this was before suitcases had wheels) only to discover that when it was winter in Fort Worth, it was stifling hot in Saigon and so humid that once off the plane I began sweating so profusely that I discovered sweat stains on the tops of my leather shoes.

I was the first *Star-Telegram* reporter to go overseas since World War II, so there was no one to meet me. I hailed a tiny cab, the driver tied my suitcase to the roof and I told him to take me to Saigon.

"You in Saigon," he told me in broken English. "Where you go in Saigon?"

I had no idea. I had come to Vietnam to cover the war and realized I had no idea where it was.

By dark, I found the Associated Press bureau and Ed White, the bureau chief (and kindest man I ever knew), found me a place to stay, told me how to get credentials, and by the end of the week I was in the field, tracking down the Fort Worth kids I had come to write about.

As I look back on it, my arrival in Saigon very much paralleled America's entry to Vietnam, a war that had been going on long before many Americans realized there was such a place.

I had gone there as a brash young hawk. I had come of age during the cold war with the Soviet Union, confident that a country that could win World War II could win any war. The government had been telling us that once and for all we had to draw a line and tell the communists they could not cross it. Better to draw that line in Vietnam than on our own shores. That seemed right to me.

Once there, I realized it was not so simple. So it was with America's leaders. It took me a while to find the war; it took them longer to understand what it was about.

Six weeks later, on an operation with Marines and South Vietnamese forces near Da Nang, I realized that whatever our good intentions, this was not going to work. When the captain gave the order to move out, the Vietnamese troops refused to go. They made various excuses, then finally just set down.

It seems obvious in retrospect, but I understood for the first time that although we could help the Vietnamese, this was their war and we couldn't do it for them. What I was coming to understand was that these soldiers had been fighting long before we got there and they were tired of war, tired of the corruption that plagued their military. Maybe they were right to feel that way, but if that's how they felt, how could we help them? The farmers in the countryside were even less motivated: We thought we were fighting communists; all the farmers knew was that people had been coming through their villages for years with guns. They did whatever the people with guns told them to do. What I didn't understand was why the people in Washington didn't see what I was seeing. And before we fully understood what was happening, nearly 60,000 Americans would die.

SCHIEFFER then (opposite, center) and now.

As it always is in war, no matter what the historians later decide about its rightness or wrongness, the dead remain dead and the limbs once lost do not grow back.

This remarkable book tells in word and picture the tragic story of how we finally came to understand what going to Vietnam had wrought—both there and here at home—and the tragic price we would pay.

We see in this book Vietnam before America got there, the war we fought and the chaos back home at the 1968 Democratic Convention in Chicago when opposition to the war boiled over into a deadly riot. By chance I was there, and I remember wondering if the whole country was coming apart.

It did not, but I will always believe it came very close.

I found the final irony when I returned to Vietnam as a tourist in 1997. I found a thriving country that was emerging as a regional power where Americans were welcomed.

In part because of groundbreaking diplomacy by former Vietnam prisoners of war like Senator John McCain, who returned there to reconcile with the government that had tortured him, Vietnam was becoming America's ally and wanted America's friendship.

We had gained through forgiveness what we had been unable to change with our weapons.

When I had been in Vietnam during the war many Vietnamese spoke French as a second language, and in 1997 I remember asking our guide if that was still the case.

"Only my grandmother," he said. "We all speak English now."

This book is the story of how that came to be.

Bob Schieffer is chief Washington correspondent for CBS News and moderator of Face the Nation.

The American involvement in Vietnam was confusing from the start. It would only get more confusing and disheartening as the years passed, but even at the outset, we didn't really know what we were doing or even whom we were backing. It might seem logical that, more than a half century later and with hundreds of histories having been written, all would be clear. But, no—in retrospect there is still confusion.

Many Americans might know that there was a French war in Vietnam before there was ours, a quagmire that we more or less inherited and negotiated for reasons other than those of the French. France, of course, had been one of Western Europe's great colonizers, along with the Netherlands, Portugal, Spain and England. Among France's holdings in Indochina were Vietnam, Cambodia and Laos, and in the post–World War II years, France sought to secure these lands even as nationalist movements and uprisings tore at the prewar fabric. (continued on page 15)

LIBRARY OF CONGRESS

IN EARLY 1937, much of Europe had its eyes on the Nazi rise in Germany, but France was concerned as well with controlling its Far Eastern colonial empire. Right: Native troops, in March of that year, practicing war maneuvers in a Vietnamese rice paddy. Above: This group photograph is an extraordinary document of an extraordinary summit, held in Vietnam in September 1945. U.S. OSS men on a secret mission have touched down in Vietnam and are engaging with—and coaching—the Vietminh, including (standing, third from left) the leader Ho Chi Minh with his second-in-command, in the white suit, minister of the interior in the provisional government, known by the code name "Mr. Van" but better known to history as the North Vietnamese general Vo Nguyen Giap. This rare photograph (which, like the one of them on the pages immediately following, was made by an unknown photographer) is housed in the Library of Congress and offers firm evidence of a historic cooperation between America and the Vietminh that, in retrospect, seems all but unbelievable. Henry Prunier, one member of the OSS team, who is quoted in our text, is standing behind Giap. Prunier remembered that Ho modeled his nation's declaration of independence, which was crafted in this period, on America's own. As we turn the pages of our book, we will find no more pictures of cooperation between the United States and Vietnam's communist nationalists, who were unable to persuade the OSS agents' sponsors in Washington to support further efforts against the French.

AP

Where was America in mid-1945? In a happy place, certainly, with the Second Great War being won. Vis-à-vis Vietnam, a few things that were happening there can scarcely be believed all these years later.

In July of that year, seven U.S. Office of Strategic Services (OSS) operatives parachuted into a village 75 miles northwest of Hanoi. Their top-secret mission was to train 200 guerrillas who were fighting for the four-year-old national independence force, called the Vietminh, in how to use the weaponry that America was about to give them. The Americans wanted the guerrillas to help fight the Japanese who were occupying Indochina. And the guerrillas wanted the weapons as well for their fight against the French. The

U.S. agents met with Ho Chi Minh, the Vietminh leader, and taught his right-hand man, then known as "Mr. Van" and later as General Vo Nguyen Giap, how to lob grenades overhand and launch mortars. "One time, he looked down the barrel of the mortar," remembered OSS Deer Team member Henry Prunier, who died in 2013, in an interview with the *Worcester (Massachusetts) Telegram & Gazette* in 2011. "I was shocked. His head could have been blown off."

Although Ho, Giap and the others learned their lessons well, their lobbying efforts to recruit the U.S. fully to their side against the French—Ho regaled Prunier, a Massachusetts native, with stories of his visits to Boston and even offered pretty women to the Americans (an offer declined)—would not ultimately pan out. The United States soon enough decided it would side with the French because, after all, the Vietnamese were aligned with communism. Some historians say that had that brief moment of Vietnamese–U.S. amity been enlarged upon, all the heartbreak and horror that followed could have been averted. Others say that the Red threat was so predominant in the postwar years that any such alignment was impossible.

Henry Prunier always appreciated how confusing it all was—and would remain. "It's odd," he said. "I'm a hero over there."

"UNCLE HO," as President Ho Chi Minh was called, and General Vo Nguyen Giap (with him on the left, opposite) were beloved throughout much of Vietnam. Here they're shown shortly after Ho reads the Declaration of Independence of the Democratic Republic of Vietnam, modeled after Thomas Jefferson's document, to 500,000 people in a Hanoi square. After the First Indochina War begins, with the French fighting to continue colonial rule, daily existence carries on as it was, with (clockwise from top left) oxen pulling carts down the street; members of the Cao Dai sect worshipping in their ornate oratory; children playing in a park. All the normalcy would soon change.

JACK BIRNS/LIFE (3)

AS THE FIGHTING SPREADS into a wide area of southern Indochina, members of a French machine gun crew aim their weapons from a Hanoi rooftop (above) and Ho Chi Minh presides over a session of the Council of Ministers (bottom). Right: Parisian construction workers demonstrate against the war in April 1949. Protests would go hand-in-glove with the Vietnam wars.

EVER CIVILIZED, even during war, the French set a proper table for an officers' dinner amid the fighting (below) and gather at a local pub (bottom). Both photos were taken in 1950, the same year U.S. President Harry Truman authorizes $15 million in military aid for the French, which helps pay for the armored vehicles (left) making their way through the delta. American spending will rise to $3 billion over the next four years as the U.S. finances 80 percent of the French war effort.

CARL MYDANS/LIFE

HOWARD SOCHUREK/LIFE (2)

FROM A HUMBLE BACKGROUND and with a father who raised him to hate the French, the man born Nguyen Sinh Cung studied the works of Karl Marx and took his inspiration from the Russian Revolution. Around the time he founded the Democratic Republic of Vietnam in 1945, he changed his name to Ho Chi Minh, which means "the Enlightener." In March 1951, he reads in a grotto (above, right) and is cheered by his jubilant followers (right) as the Vietminh are incorporated into another nationalist group, the Lien Viet. Opposite: In a photograph by LIFE's Carl Mydans, a French police officer searches a group of children and asks them about their dead fathers. Many of the photos in this book, even the ones from this early period, were made for LIFE. Mydans, who was held for part of World War II in a Japanese prisoner of war camp and had then recorded MacArthur coming ashore, was assigned to cover Vietnam. So was David Douglas Duncan. They would soon be joined by the magazine's next generation—Burrows, Schutzer, Rentmeester, Dominis, Olson et al.

DAVID DOUGLAS DUNCAN was already a storied LIFE photographer, having become famous for his coverage of the Korean War. But the 16-page photo essay he files for the August 3, 1953, issue, titled "Indochina, All But Lost" and shot during eight weeks on the ground, becomes one of the most noteworthy—and prescient—the magazine will ever publish. In many of the photos here and on the next pages, he portrays "a time of fear and worry" for the warring region—a time when the ancient (symbolized by the snake, opposite, in Luang Prabang, Laos) is at risk of being lost to the modern (the Grand Monde casino in Saigon, above, left, and a French billboard, below). With his depiction of lazy French staff officers, widespread corruption, opium trafficking and dead Vietnamese, "the issue almost provoked an international incident," as Russell Miller wrote in *Magnum: Fifty Years at the Front Line of History*. (Please see more about this in Duncan's words on page 30.) LIFE would later advocate for American intervention in the conflict—and later still, with the realization that the U.S. was in a quagmire with no escape, be a leading voice for the nation's changing mood.

"EVERYPLACE YOU GO
there is something to photograph
in a war," Duncan says, years
after his time in Vietnam. "You
can't miss it." Here, he presents
a Saigon golf course through
a barbed-wire fence in 1951 (left)
and children playing soccer in
front of an ancient tomb in Laos
in 1953 (opposite). They are
wrought photographs describing
a quickly changing landscape.
David Douglas Duncan is today
fewer than two years shy of his
hundredth birthday, and from
his home in the south of France
he recalls, in a sentiment similar
to that voiced by Bob Schieffer
in our foreword, "Vietnam was
so different from World War II.
I was one of the first guys in.
In 1950, by September, we
started bringing in troops—and
there just was no training. They
simply weren't soldiers going in.
Vietnam, it was a screw-up from
the early stages. I went back
for LIFE in '53, and the programs
just weren't working. You could
see it if you were there."

DUNCAN CAPTURED SCENES both ordinary (a woman in an alleyway, top left) and extraordinary (a man, top right, with a shattered shoulder, who exudes "smoldering resentment," as Duncan wrote; and a "nearly blind peasant and family" who risked the Vietminh's wrath by moving into a U.S.–sponsored housing project, opposite). Duncan's shots taken inside an opium den (above, left and right) seem to show people, as he wrote in his book *Photo Nomad,* who, "lost in their toxic Dantean escape with opium, shared dreams—maybe Ho Chi Minh's."

THE WAR INTENSIFIES as the United States steps up its involvement. In 1945 it consisted of seven OSS men training a relatively few Vietminh guerrillas, but now, in 1953, a steady stream of money and supplies flows in to support the French—the other side, and the side the U.S. will stick to. On these pages: Vietnamese bystanders view a parade under a recruiting poster (opposite); units of a new national army march through the streets of Hanoi carrying weapons purchased with U.S. military aid (above); and Americans and French, both, inspect newly arrived ambulances (right).

"**INDOCHINA, ALL BUT LOST**" was the name of the astonishingly before-its-time feature that ran in LIFE in 1953, with David Douglas Duncan's photographs and, indeed, his reportage. His words to accompany this picture: "From a heartbroken widow I heard cries come in the high-pitched accents of the East." The stone at right marks the grave of her husband, Pham-Ngoc-Linh, who had "died for France." As Duncan explains, "The sad fact is that twice as many Indochinese [died] in France's war as Frenchmen." And, of course, many more Vietnamese— civilians and combatants—than Americans would die in the next Indochinese war. Duncan today well remembers the furor his startling story caused in the halls of Time Inc. in 1953 after the French Foreign Ministry called the company's über-boss Henry Luce on the carpet for "defamation and slander": "I had gone up to the northern border. I had shot what was happening. By chance, [Edward Thompson, LIFE's managing editor] was in Paris, and in New York the story ran. The [expletive] hit the fan. Luce was really perturbed. I was really tired. Basically, the bottom line was, 'If you don't like it, fire me.' He'd fired Teddy White over China. He didn't fire me. But I had been a Marine and was perfectly satisfied in my opinions of warfare. He didn't have those opinions."

DAVID DOUGLAS DUNCAN/LIFE

ICI REPOSE
PHAM-NGOC-LINH
PARTISAN
3/6 R.I.C
MORT POUR LA FRANCE
20-6-50

REALITY SETS IN as the number of casualties climbs and it becomes clear just what *kind* of war is being fought. During a French attack on the Vietminh in December 1953, barefoot troops carry their equipment on their shoulders (below) and a Vietminh soldier is routed from an underground tunnel (bottom). Right: Women and children walk through a muddy swamp, three dead Vietminh soldiers in view.

HOWARD SOCHUREK/LIFE (3)

AFTER A TWO-MONTH BATTLE at Dien Bien Phu led by a brilliant General Giap, the outnumbered, outmaneuvered French (shown below, left, and bottom left and right) surrender to the Vietminh on May 7, 1954, after a total of 400,000 troops and civilians have been killed. In the aftermath of France's withdrawal, the communist victors enter Hanoi (below) as many residents flee the city (opposite). The anticommunist prime minister of the newly created South Vietnam, Ngo Dinh Diem, predicts—correctly—"another, more deadly war" in Vietnam's future.

DURING WORLD WAR II, LIFE's large deployment of photographers had suffered grievous harm—Eugene Smith was nearly killed after being hit by mortar fire at Okinawa; Carl Mydans was imprisoned by the Japanese—but no one had died. In Indochina, the fate of this storied team turned. LIFE suffered a great tragedy on May 25, 1954, when the 40-year-old Hungarian-born photographer Robert Capa, who had landed with the first wave of troops on D-Day (his few surviving images for LIFE, now classics, would much later inform the look of Steven Spielberg's *Saving Private Ryan*), was killed. He had been asked by LIFE to travel from Japan to Vietnam to make a report on the increasingly disturbing situation there and had stepped on a land mine. At bottom left is one of the very last photographs Capa ever shot: of Vietnamese troops advancing, slowly, between Nam Dinh and Thai Binh. Opposite: Capa's casket is borne toward the aircraft that will take him home. David Douglas Duncan remembers that the photographers didn't really have an agenda, particularly at that time. "I never thought about it," he says, describing the political situation. "I was rolling with the punches my whole life." And so had Capa been. But in the year he was killed—1954—the situation in Vietnam was changing greatly. The French were being defeated, and a lull was ensuing that would not last. At left, top: French troops pay their last respects to their fallen comrades prior to leaving Hanoi. Middle left: South Vietnamese prime minister Ngo Dinh Diem, center, talks with U.S. Secretary of State John Foster Dulles in Saigon as the United States becomes the new major player. Middle right: The glamorous Vietnamese femme fatale Madame Ngo Dinh Nhu, Diem's sister-in-law, becomes the de facto first lady of South Vietnam and a dragon lady prototype to be propagated by Western media—including LIFE—in the next several years.

WHEN VIETNAM IS DIVIDED into North and South in the Geneva Accords, Ho Chi Minh returns to Hanoi after eight years in the jungle to take official control of North Vietnam. At right, he visits the front in 1958; below, his troops in training. Opposite, top: A photo by John Dominis, one of the early LIFE photographers to report from Vietnam, shows an American volunteer helping a farmer in a field. Below: President John F. Kennedy and Nguyen Dinh Thuan, secretary of state of South Vietnam, discuss the communist threat. So, then: on the left page, the Vietminh's gathering confidence. On the right page, America's tentative but increasing engagement.

APIC/HULTON/GETTY

JOHN DOMINIS/LIFE (2)

BETTMANN/CORBIS

A PRESIDENT UNDER INCREASING PRESSURE from the State Department and the Pentagon to deploy combat troops to Vietnam, Kennedy in October 1961 announces at a press conference that he is sending General Maxwell Taylor to assess the situation (right). "The President made it abundantly clear that he fervently hoped the necessary military force could be provided by the Vietnamese without the need to introduce U.S. ground troops into combat," Taylor later wrote. "I assured him that I shared that hope . . . but a government had to be willing to do the unpalatable when necessary in the national interest." Opposite: The general, seated at center, in Vietnam later that month.

AMERICA'S VIETNAM

We offer here a timeline and statistical analysis of the United States's involvement in the Southeast Asian conflict, including events important to America's cold war face-off with communism, as compiled by LIFE's Amy Lennard Goehner.

2/20 John Glenn becomes the first U.S. astronaut to orbit the earth.

10/16–28 After the U.S. discovers the Soviet Union building missile sites in Cuba, JFK orders a ring of ships to surround the island, preventing supplies from being delivered. For 13 days the threat of nuclear war looms during the Cuban Missile Crisis. As the world holds its breath, President Kennedy and Soviet premier Nikita Khrushchev come to an agreement.

8/7 The Gulf of Tonkin Resolution is passed, giving LBJ broader power to use force in Vietnam. It was drafted in reaction to alleged attacks by North Vietnamese torpedo boats on American ships in the gulf.

8/26 Lyndon B. Johnson is chosen as the Democratic Party's candidate for President and selects Minnesota senator Hubert Humphrey as his running mate.

11/3 LBJ wins the presidential election with a landslide victory over Arizona senator Barry Goldwater.

DECEMBER Nearly 400,000 U.S. servicemen are engaged in Vietnam by year's end.

> **AVERAGE NUMBER OF DAYS U.S. INFANTRYMEN IN VIETNAM SAW COMBAT: 240**
>
> **AVERAGE NUMBER OF DAYS U.S. INFANTRYMEN SERVING IN THE SOUTH PACIFIC DURING WORLD WAR II SAW COMBAT: 40**

> **AMOUNT OF AGENT ORANGE HERBICIDE USED BY THE U.S.: 13 MILLION GALLONS**

| 1961 | 1962 | 1963 | 1964 | 1965 | 1966 | 1967 |

1/17 Ending his presidential term, Dwight D. Eisenhower warns of the "military-industrial complex."

1/20 John F. Kennedy is sworn in as the 35th U.S. President.

4/12 Soviet cosmonaut Yuri Gagarin orbits the earth.

4/17 In an attempt to overthrow Cuban dictator Fidel Castro, some 1,400 U.S.–trained Cuban exiles land on the island and are defeated in the Bay of Pigs invasion.

MAY JFK sends 500 Special Forces troops and military advisers to Vietnam.

8/10 The U.S. first uses the defoliant Agent Orange to destroy crops and jungle foliage being used by the enemy for camouflage.

8/13 The communist East German government builds the Berlin Wall, halting massive emigration to the democratic West.

12/22 Specialist 4 James T. Davis becomes the first American battlefield fatality in Vietnam.

6/20 The U.S. and Russia agree to establish a hotline ensuring quick communication.

6/26 JFK visits West Berlin and declares, *"Ich bin ein Berliner"* ("I am a Berliner"), acknowledging his support for the democratic West.

8/5 The U.S., the United Kingdom and the Soviet Union sign the Nuclear Test Ban Treaty, prohibiting testing nuclear weapons except underground.

9/10 JFK exempts married men from the military draft.

11/22 President Kennedy is assassinated while riding in a motorcade in Dallas, Texas. Lyndon Baines Johnson is sworn in later that day aboard Air Force One.

3/8 Three thousand five hundred U.S. Marines reach the beaches of Vietnam, becoming the first troops sent over for combat.

7/28 LBJ commits 50,000 troops to Vietnam, which will increase the U.S. forces to 125,000. Monthly draft calls double in size to 35,000.

10/15 During a demonstration headed by the National Coordinating Committee to End the War in Vietnam, a young Catholic pacifist becomes the first protestor to publicly burn his draft card.

NOVEMBER As the war intensifies in Vietnam, U.S. casualties hit a record of 240 troops killed and 470 wounded in one week.

1/15 At Yale University, 462 faculty members send President Johnson a letter calling for an end to the bombing of North Vietnam. Faculty at other universities follow suit.

1/27 Three U.S. astronauts are killed in a flash fire during a simulation of their upcoming Apollo 1 flight.

2/15 Two thousand five hundred women go to the Pentagon and demand to see "the generals who send our sons to die."

3/6 LBJ announces plan to reform the draft and create a lottery.

3/26 Ten thousand hippies stage a nonviolent "Be-In" in Central Park.

4/17 World heavyweight boxing champion Muhammad Ali refuses induction into military service and is stripped of his boxing crown. He will be sentenced to five years in jail and fined $10,000 for draft evasion; the conviction is later overturned by the U.S. Supreme Court.

10/21 Writer Norman Mailer is among the protestors in a march on the Pentagon.

> **NUMBER OF SOUTH VIETNAMESE TROOPS KILLED: 200,000–250,000**
>
> **NUMBER OF NORTH VIETNAMESE AND VIETCONG TROOPS KILLED: 1.1 MILLION**
>
> **NUMBER OF SOUTH AND NORTH VIETNAMESE CIVILIAN DEATHS: 2 MILLION**

FEBRUARY Referring to the Tet Offensive, in which the North Vietnamese launch a massive series of attacks throughout South Vietnam, Senator Robert F. Kennedy says, "A total military victory is not within sight or around the corner; in fact, it is probably beyond our grasp."

3/16 Robert F. Kennedy enters the presidential race.

3/16 In one of the war's worst atrocities against unarmed civilians, American soldiers massacre between 300 and 500 civilians, many of them women and children, in the village of My Lai.

3/31 LBJ announces he will end bombing of North Vietnam and says he will not seek reelection.

APRIL In the wake of the Tet Offensive, Secretary of Defense Clark Clifford announces a call-up of 24,500 reservists and National Guardsmen.

4/4 Dr. Martin Luther King Jr., 39, is shot to death on his motel balcony in Memphis, Tennessee.

NUMBER OF AMERICANS WHO SERVED IN SOUTHEAST ASIA DURING THE VIETNAM WAR: 3.3 MILLION

PEAK FORCE: 543,400

4/20 President Nixon announces 150,000 American troops will be withdrawn from South Vietnam.

4/30 President Nixon stuns Americans by announcing he will send combat troops to North Vietnamese-controlled areas of Cambodia, assuring the nation, "Once enemy forces are driven out . . . we will withdraw."

5/4 Ohio National Guardsmen fire into a crowd at Kent State University during an antiwar demonstration, killing four students and wounding nine. The killings shock the nation and result in student strikes throughout the country.

6/29 The last U.S. troops pull out of Cambodia.

FEBRUARY Senator Edward Kennedy of Massachusetts calls for draft resisters to be granted amnesty. President Nixon visits China and meets with Mao Zedong and Premier Chou Enlai.

MARCH U.S. announces suspension of Paris Peace Talks.

6/28 President Nixon announces that no new draftees will be sent to Vietnam unless they volunteer.

JULY Actress Jane Fonda travels to North Vietnam and poses for a photograph on an antiaircraft gun, earning the sobriquet "Hanoi Jane."

10/26 U.S. national security adviser Henry Kissinger declares, "Peace is at hand" in Vietnam.

DECEMBER Nixon orders massive bombing of North Vietnam.

1969

1968

Race riots supplant antiwar demonstrations in major cities.

4/23 Columbia University students, led by Students for a Democratic Society leader Mark Rudd, barricade the office of the dean. Similar protests take place at colleges and high schools.

MAY The U.S. and North Vietnam begin preliminary peace talks in Paris, with the goal of ending the war. And some 2,000 servicemen are killed in Vietnam during the month, a new record.

6/5 Presidential candidate Robert F. Kennedy is fatally shot in L.A.

8/26–8/29 Police and antiwar demonstrators clash at the Democratic National Convention in Chicago. The chant "The whole world is watching" is heard by millions of television viewers.

10/23 Students at the University of California, Berkeley, seize an office building on campus.

11/6 Richard Nixon is elected President, defeating Democratic candidate Hubert Humphrey.

1970

MARCH President Nixon threatens to resume bombing of North Vietnam.

4/3 U.S. deaths in Vietnam, now at 33,641, outnumber the total of servicemen killed in the Korean War.

4/4 CBS cancels *The Smothers Brothers Comedy Hour* because of its controversial criticism of the war.

7/20 Astronauts Neil Armstrong and Edwin "Buzz" Aldrin land on the moon, Armstrong declaring, "That's one small step for a man, one giant leap for mankind."

10/15 In the Vietnam Moratorium, the largest antiwar demonstration to date, millions of Americans of all ages march in cities throughout the nation.

NUMBER OF U.S. WOMEN STATIONED IN COMBAT ZONES ALONGSIDE THEIR BROTHER TROOPS: MORE THAN 10,000

1971

1972

4/10 In what is dubbed Ping-Pong diplomacy, players from the U.S. table-tennis team play exhibition matches in mainland China, becoming the first Americans to visit that country since the communist takeover in 1949.

APRIL Members of Vietnam Veterans Against the War throw away their medals at a protest on Capitol Hill in Washington.

JUNE *The New York Times* begins printing the Pentagon Papers, a secret Defense Department document outlining the U.S. role in Vietnam, which had been leaked to the newspaper. Nixon tries unsuccessfully to halt publication.

10/25 The U.N. General Assembly votes to admit the People's Republic of China.

1973

JANUARY President Nixon claims that a Vietnam peace plan has been signed in Paris and that U.S. prisoners of war will be released.

3/29 The last United States combat troops leave South Vietnam, ending America's direct military involvement in the war.

NUMBER OF AMERICANS KILLED: MORE THAN 58,000

AMERICAN AID TO SOUTH VIETNAM: $24 BILLION

TEN CRUCIAL BATTLES

JANUARY 2 1963	NOVEMBER 1965	JANUARY TO MARCH 1968	JANUARY TO MARCH 1968	MAY 1969

THE BATTLE OF AP BAC

In January 1963, the South Vietnamese set out to attack a Vietcong (VC) radio station in the hamlet of Ap Bac, southwest of Saigon. With U.S. Lieutenant Colonel John Vann as a senior adviser to the Army of the Republic of Vietnam (ARVN), a few dozen Americans led a force of infantry and helicopters on a three-pronged attack. The army had a huge superiority, and even the VC commander expected to be beaten, admitting in his diary, "Better to fight and die than run and be slaughtered." Yet the South's leadership was cowardly, and when the VC learned of the attack they beefed up their defenses with battle-hardened soldiers setting up along a tree-lined canal that offered cover and shooting down American helicopters. ARVN paratroopers landed in the wrong spot, troops would not advance under fire and an armored commander delayed rescuing the men. When he did, the VC destroyed his vehicles. The communists then easily slipped away. And while the Americans called Ap Bac a success, Vann deemed the assault "a miserable damn performance, just like always."

THE BATTLE OF IA DRANG VALLEY

This, the first major fight between regular U.S. and the People's Army of Vietnam (PAVN) forces, took place in the Central Highlands' Ia Drang Valley. Learning that there were enemies in the jungle, Lieutenant Colonel Harold Moore brought in a flock of UH-1 Huey helicopters. The landing spot, with its elephant grass and tall anthills, proved too small to bring in more than eight choppers at a time, so artillery had to lay down cover fire as they landed. Other forces joined them, and patrols headed out to sweep the area. But instead of the expected small band of PAVN troops, there were closer to 1,600 occupying the hills. As casualties mounted and supplies dwindled, the Americans struggled to keep the area open. Bitter assaults continued, and artillery units and B-52 bombers raced in. By the end of the battle, the Americans had lost more than 300 men, with the PAVN losing more than 3,500. The U.S. saw the lopsided body count as a positive sign, and the assault proved the effectiveness of air mobility. But the confrontation also emboldened the North Vietnamese, who realized they had a fighting chance if they could keep close to the enemy so that the U.S. could not use artillery barrages or air assaults without sacrificing their own men. It was a method of fighting they embraced going forward.

THE BATTLE OF KHE SANH

The Americans learned that the enemy was massing troops near their remote Khe Sanh outpost on the Laotian border. Fearing that an assault would turn into another Dien Bien Phu—the 1954 battle in which the communists ended France's colonial rule—the Americans determined to strengthen their position. Marine Colonel David Lownds oversaw the increase of manpower to 6,000 Marines and a battalion of South Vietnamese rangers, who stockpiled supplies and shored up defenses. An airstrip was built, trenches dug, bunkers constructed. Up to 40,000 North Vietnamese in the surrounding jungle also formed trenches and threw up bunkers. Rockets and mortars started raining in on the morning of January 21. The communists made regular assaults, and President Lyndon Johnson was so interested in the outcome that he had a model of the base brought into the White House Situation Room. The 77-day siege proved to be one of the bloodiest battles of the war.

THE TET OFFENSIVE

General Vo Nguyen Giap, who had successfully ousted the French, was determined to do the same to the Americans. He had tunnels and chambers set up around major South Vietnamese cities and filled them with supplies in time for the celebration of Tet, the Vietnamese New Year. As citizens traveled to visit their families, soldiers dressed as civilians slipped into the cities. Then on January 30, VC and PAVN troops set out on a coordinated attack, swarming into five major cities, three dozen provincial capitals and more than 60 district capitals. The Americans, who had been preoccupied with Khe Sanh to the north, were overwhelmed by the severity of the Tet Offensive, which destroyed airfields and exploded fuel depots. In Saigon the VC attacked the Presidential Palace and breached the outer wall of the U.S. embassy. Despite the enthusiasm of the VC and PAVN fighters, they were ill prepared for the crushing American response. Although the allies won the fight, the trauma of the battle and the negative press coverage of Tet and Khe Sanh turned public opinion against the war. Brigadier General S.L.A. Marshall summed up the Tet Offensive in these words: "A potential major victory turned into a disastrous defeat through mistaken estimates, loss of nerve and a tidal wave of defeatism."

THE BATTLE OF HAMBURGER HILL

Ap Bia Mountain in the A Shau Valley along the Laotian border translates as "the mountain of the crouching beast," and feral brutality sprung from there in the spring of 1969. The mountain has a number of large ridges, among them what the Americans prosaically called Hill 937, and the communists used the area to squirrel away supplies along that part of the Ho Chi Minh Trail—an intricate route of jungle and mountain trails and paths. In May 1969, Operation Apache Snow was set in motion to clear out the enemy. Huey helicopters and Cobra gunships swooped in, and assaulting Americans blanketed the hill, spider holes, trenches, bunkers and tunnels with mortars, artillery and napalm. Snipers retaliated by picking off the troops and dropping grenades on them from the jungle canopy. By the time the Americans conquered the charred mound 10 days later, it had become one of the war's bloodiest encounters. The battle was compared to a human meat grinder, and one of the troops nailed a sign to a burnt stump dubbing the spot "Hamburger Hill." Another sign asked the question, "Was it worth it?"

During the decade of American fighting in Vietnam, there were several confrontations of more violence or consequence than others, as LIFE's Daniel S. Levy explains.

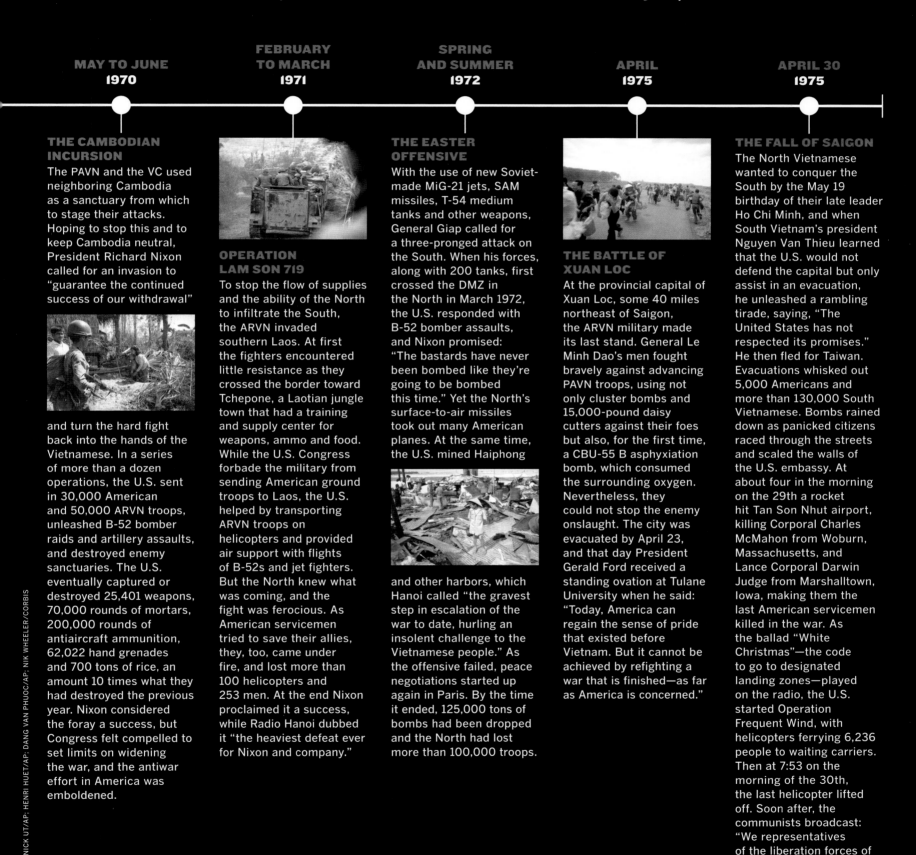

| MAY TO JUNE 1970 | FEBRUARY TO MARCH 1971 | SPRING AND SUMMER 1972 | APRIL 1975 | APRIL 30 1975 |

THE CAMBODIAN INCURSION

The PAVN and the VC used neighboring Cambodia as a sanctuary from which to stage their attacks. Hoping to stop this and to keep Cambodia neutral, President Richard Nixon called for an invasion to "guarantee the continued success of our withdrawal"

and turn the hard fight back into the hands of the Vietnamese. In a series of more than a dozen operations, the U.S. sent in 30,000 American and 50,000 ARVN troops, unleashed B-52 bomber raids and artillery assaults, and destroyed enemy sanctuaries. The U.S. eventually captured or destroyed 25,401 weapons, 70,000 rounds of mortars, 200,000 rounds of antiaircraft ammunition, 62,022 hand grenades and 700 tons of rice, an amount 10 times what they had destroyed the previous year. Nixon considered the foray a success, but Congress felt compelled to set limits on widening the war, and the antiwar effort in America was emboldened.

OPERATION LAM SON 719

To stop the flow of supplies and the ability of the North to infiltrate the South, the ARVN invaded southern Laos. At first the fighters encountered little resistance as they crossed the border toward Tchepone, a Laotian jungle town that had a training and supply center for weapons, ammo and food. While the U.S. Congress forbade the military from sending American ground troops to Laos, the U.S. helped by transporting ARVN troops on helicopters and provided air support with flights of B-52s and jet fighters. But the North knew what was coming, and the fight was ferocious. As American servicemen tried to save their allies, they, too, came under fire, and lost more than 100 helicopters and 253 men. At the end Nixon proclaimed it a success, while Radio Hanoi dubbed it "the heaviest defeat ever for Nixon and company."

THE EASTER OFFENSIVE

With the use of new Soviet-made MiG-21 jets, SAM missiles, T-54 medium tanks and other weapons, General Giap called for a three-pronged attack on the South. When his forces, along with 200 tanks, first crossed the DMZ in the North in March 1972, the U.S. responded with B-52 bomber assaults, and Nixon promised: "The bastards have never been bombed like they're going to be bombed this time." Yet the North's surface-to-air missiles took out many American planes. At the same time, the U.S. mined Haiphong

and other harbors, which Hanoi called "the gravest step in escalation of the war to date, hurling an insolent challenge to the Vietnamese people." As the offensive failed, peace negotiations started up again in Paris. By the time it ended, 125,000 tons of bombs had been dropped and the North had lost more than 100,000 troops.

THE BATTLE OF XUAN LOC

At the provincial capital of Xuan Loc, some 40 miles northeast of Saigon, the ARVN military made its last stand. General Le Minh Dao's men fought bravely against advancing PAVN troops, using not only cluster bombs and 15,000-pound daisy cutters against their foes but also, for the first time, a CBU-55 B asphyxiation bomb, which consumed the surrounding oxygen. Nevertheless, they could not stop the enemy onslaught. The city was evacuated by April 23, and that day President Gerald Ford received a standing ovation at Tulane University when he said: "Today, America can regain the sense of pride that existed before Vietnam. But it cannot be achieved by refighting a war that is finished—as far as America is concerned."

THE FALL OF SAIGON

The North Vietnamese wanted to conquer the South by the May 19 birthday of their late leader Ho Chi Minh, and when South Vietnam's president Nguyen Van Thieu learned that the U.S. would not defend the capital but only assist in an evacuation, he unleashed a rambling tirade, saying, "The United States has not respected its promises." He then fled for Taiwan. Evacuations whisked out 5,000 Americans and more than 130,000 South Vietnamese. Bombs rained down as panicked citizens raced through the streets and scaled the walls of the U.S. embassy. At about four in the morning on the 29th a rocket hit Tan Son Nhut airport, killing Corporal Charles McMahon from Woburn, Massachusetts, and Lance Corporal Darwin Judge from Marshalltown, Iowa, making them the last American servicemen killed in the war. As the ballad "White Christmas"—the code to go to designated landing zones—played on the radio, the U.S. started Operation Frequent Wind, with helicopters ferrying 6,236 people to waiting carriers. Then at 7:53 on the morning of the 30th, the last helicopter lifted off. Soon after, the communists broadcast: "We representatives of the liberation forces of Saigon formally proclaim that Saigon had been totally liberated."

TALKING WAR

One man served in the Vietnam War and later became a college professor. In that role he mentored many, including a student who would fight for the United States in Iraq. Paul Miles and Nate Rawlings recently reunited and talked for this LIFE book about their experiences of modern war.

Paul Miles, a history professor at Princeton until he retired in 2014, experienced Vietnam from the beginning of the war till long past the bitter end, and he would spend much of his later career examining the lessons of that war. Miles was a 1960 graduate of West Point and later won a Rhodes Scholarship to study modern history at Christ Church, Oxford, in England. In early 1965, he took command of the largest engineer company in the U.S. Army and deployed with his troops to Vietnam. For 13 months, his company executed reconnaissance missions, constructed the massive military base at Cam Rahn Bay, and built dozens of smaller logistical hubs up and down South Vietnam's central coast—lifelines for the half million troops who would fight in the country at the height of the war.

After his combat tour, Miles served as an aide-de-camp to General William Westmoreland, the Army Chief of Staff who had commanded American troops in Vietnam from 1964 until 1968. In the summer of 1972, while the majority of Americans were leaving Vietnam, Miles returned for a second tour. He served as a member of the U.S. military delegation to the Paris peace talks, then returned to Vietnam as part of a small staff who implemented the final cease-fire. He volunteered to remain behind to negotiate for the return of troops missing in action and left Vietnam for the last time in late 1973.

Nate Rawlings, one of Miles's former Princeton students, is a veteran of the Iraq War. Eventually reaching the rank of captain and leading an embedded combat adviser team to the Iraqi Army, he completed two tours of duty, serving from 2005 to 2009. A former writer for *Time* and now a special adviser to the undersecretary for public diplomacy and public affairs at the U.S. Department of State, Rawlings acknowledges that his thoughts on war, particularly in the modern age, have been influenced by those of his former teacher.

Here, those thoughts, especially regarding Vietnam, are shared, with Rawlings representing LIFE.

LIFE: You've written and lectured about historians' challenges as they wrestle with Vietnam, and one of those is basic chronology. There are several arguments about when the war began, and there isn't even a clear consensus about the end. Why do we have so much trouble defining the parameters of the Vietnam War?
MILES: With the exception of the Civil War, there is no chapter in

American history that better illustrates Dutch historian Pieter Geyl's aphorism "History is an argument without end." Even if we measure the chronological scope of the war in the narrowest terms—the period when American military forces were directly involved in combat operations—we are still talking about a war that lasted almost eight years. Most historians would say that the Vietnam War lasted longer than that. Some would say the war began in 1961, when President Kennedy dispatched American military advisers to South Vietnam in significant numbers—in other words, 12 years. Others would say the war began in 1955, when the United States replaced France as the sponsor of the new Republic of Vietnam—in other words, 18 years. There are also those who would say that the war began in 1950 when the Truman administration extended economic and military assistance to the French, who were fighting to retain their colonial empire in Indochina—in other words, 23 years. And finally, there are those who would argue that the war did not really end until 1975, when North Vietnamese tanks crashed through the gates of the Presidential Palace in Saigon. From that perspective, the war lasted a quarter of a century.

LIFE: If we can't even settle on when the war began and ended, how can historians grapple with the other huge questions about the war?
MILES: We continue to search for answers to the most complicated questions: Was the goal of establishing an independent, noncommunist South Vietnam a realistic undertaking, or was it doomed to failure from the start? On the other hand, if U.S. policy was not fundamentally flawed, were there alternative strategies that could have produced a different outcome? One of the most long-standing questions is, Would the American experience in Vietnam have been different if John F. Kennedy had not been assassinated? Would Kennedy have made the same fateful decisions as his successor, Lyndon Johnson? Those are questions I'm still researching to this day.

LIFE: Going back to the beginning when you were in your first assignment as a young lieutenant, we had advisers in Vietnam. Were there discussions about whether that would escalate? Was Vietnam a place you thought your career might take you?
MILES: No. The number of advisers in Vietnam in the early 1960s was very small, increasing to almost 17,000 by the time President Kennedy was assassinated. I'm sure most of my contemporaries assumed that their next assignment would be either in Germany or in Korea. I have a very vivid memory of sitting on my cot at the Ranger camp down in Florida in January 1961, listening to Kennedy's inaugural address, where he said we would "pay any price,

THE PROFESSOR: Paul Miles is seen in the rotunda of Princeton's Nassau Hall (opposite), which also serves as the university's war memorial. He earned a Ph.D. at age 61, and taught at both West Point and Princeton, but it is the years that came before—his years in the U.S. Army—that make him such an effective scholar of military and diplomatic history.

COURTESY NATE RAWLINGS

THE STUDENT: Nate Rawlings in Kandahar, Afghanistan, on assignment for *Time* in January 2011, above. He served two tours in Iraq as an Army officer after attending Princeton and later earned graduate degrees from Columbia. "One of the hardest things about coming home after combat," he said, "[is] trying to put the things you experienced into a context that makes sense for the rest of your life."

free, noncommunist South Vietnam—was not going to be achieved within a reasonable period of time and at a reasonable cost. But even more significant from my point of view, it was apparent that the Army as an institution was paying a price. By that time there were problems with discipline, problems with drugs, problems with alcohol. I subscribed to the outlook that withdrawing from Vietnam, bringing that war to some conclusion, was in our interest. And I had the impression that maybe in the long run it wasn't going to make that much of a difference with the Vietnamese. The international situation had changed. By 1972, we were in a détente with the Soviets, and it was not as if we were in Vietnam to contain communism. When you looked at the destruction of the countryside and the amount of casualties, North and South, it was hard to make the case that it could be worse with some kind of cease-fire or negotiated agreement.

bear any burden" in the defense of liberty. I was very much aware of what we might call a new direction in U.S. foreign policy. But I would not say that Vietnam loomed large in 1961.

LIFE: When you landed in Vietnam in the spring of 1965, what were your first impressions of the country?

MILES: Before my company arrived at Cam Ranh Bay, I did a bit of reconnaissance work. I went up to Quy Nhon, hitched a ride on a fixed wing aircraft and a helicopter, and I saw the great diversity in terrain. If some veteran is reminiscing about Vietnam, his story will depend on where he was. War in the delta—rice paddies, smooth as a bowling ball—was very different from the war in the central highlands, which had mountains, hills and thick jungle. Then you got all the way up to the north, where the Marines fought near the demilitarized zone, and in some places there was very open terrain. Marines were dug in with relatively fixed lines. Just flying over the country, one got the impression of how varied that element of the war would be.

One's experience in Vietnam also depended heavily on the time that person was there. The character of the war varied quite a bit depending upon whether you're talking about the early 1960s, when it was primarily an insurgency, a guerrilla war; or 1965 to 1968, when it was something of a mixture; then after 1968 all the way to 1972, it had more characteristics of a conventional war with bigger offensives and Vietnamization.

LIFE: You left Vietnam in 1966, served as an aide-de-camp to General Westmoreland at the Pentagon, and you didn't return until the summer of 1972. What had changed, both in the country and in your own views?

MILES: I guess I was what some would call a dove, having concluded at some point, maybe in 1970 or 1971, that our original goal—a

LIFE: You were serving in Saigon when you were sent to Paris toward the end of the peace talks. When the parties finally arrived at a conclusion, and the basic agreement was signed, was that it? The Vietnam War was over?

MILES: That was the beginning of the end. Once the foreign ministers signed the basic agreements in the morning, the military representatives met in the afternoon to confirm arrangements for setting up a military commission in Saigon. And more important, we exchanged lists of prisoners of war. All week, officials, reporters and the public back home were anxiously awaiting this list. We knew who had gone missing, but we didn't know who the North Vietnamese had in captivity.

The highlight of my experience in Paris came that day. A Vietcong secretary, who had been in civilian clothes for months, appeared that afternoon in military uniform. She gave me the list. I accepted the list of prisoners of war on behalf of the United States. As soon as the meeting was over, we left the Hotel Kleber, and I walked out and there was a bank of reporters. By that time, the text of the agreement had been publicized, and someone called out, "Do you have the list?" And I held it up and said, "I've got the list." We rushed to the embassy to cross-check the list with the one that we had been developing for some time.

LIFE: After the signing of the Paris Peace Accords, you returned to Saigon as part of the military commission, then you volunteered to stay behind and continue working on efforts to find service members missing in action. When you finally left Vietnam in 1973, the American experience was, for the most part, over, but the war still continued.

MILES: It did, until 1975, when the North Vietnamese finally took Saigon. I was an instructor at West Point, and at that time all three networks had a brief news program at 11:45 a.m. Once the North Vietnamese were on the march, every day I would turn it on for the last five minutes of class to get the latest report. The cadets and I saw it there, on the small television in my classroom. It was a very depressing experience. It was very difficult to put any positive spin on that.

The question I've been asked many times is whether I thought the Paris peace agreement was sound. From a military point of view, I had reservations—and the top generals had reservations—about the failure to require the total withdrawal of North Vietnamese forces from South Vietnam. They were being left on the high ground, in a position within a day's march of the old capital of Hué. Did I have reservations about the agreement? Yes. At the time, a lot of people thought that continued American airpower would make a difference. Did I think that the reintroduction of airpower would make a difference? No.

LIFE: How did the experience of Vietnam influence subsequent wars?

MILES: I'd be hard-pressed to say there was much impact on the smaller conflicts of the 1980s: Grenada and Panama. Vietnam might have reinforced the inclination to take all measures to ensure the operation would be limited and quick. But in no case were the stakes comparable to Vietnam. It was not until the Gulf War that anyone thought about the possibility of a quagmire.

In 1990, there was a significant debate over authorizing military force to evict Saddam Hussein from Kuwait. There was a significant, heated debate, and opinion was split. I listened to that debate, and there were frequent references to Vietnam. More than one senator said, "I voted for the Gulf of Tonkin resolution, and I learned my lesson." There was a little bit about that later with the Iraq War, but it was by no means comparable to feelings leading up to the Gulf War.

LIFE: What are some of the most important continuing arguments about Vietnam among historians today?

MILES: The argument most apparent among political historians is that it was a lost cause, doomed to failure. The goal was unrealistic— the idea that, in a reasonable amount of time, you could develop a functioning democratic system and a modern army in Vietnam. Those were just beyond reasonable expectations. So debates about alternate military strategy are irrelevant if the policy was flawed from the beginning.

The second school of thought is diametrically opposed. People making this argument propose alternate strategies: more bombing, earlier incursions in Cambodia and Laos, earlier emphasis on pacification, a better chain of command, better planning, and on and on— all these what-ifs. If only there had been these alternate military strategies or programs, there would have been a different outcome.

Then of course there's another argument that acknowledges that the policy was flawed, at least with respect to the goal of an independent, noncommunist South Vietnam, which was part of a broader policy of containment. Even in failure, this argument says we succeeded in drawing the line. But instead of drawing it at the 17th parallel—keeping communism out of South Vietnam—we really drew a line outside of Vietnam. The Philippines and Singapore prospered, and Indonesia did not become communist. Those subscribing to this theory see a victory in that sense.

But that really wasn't why we were in Vietnam. The reason we were in Vietnam, the reason why 500,000 American troops fought there at the height of the war, the reason there are more than 58,000 names on the Vietnam Memorial, is that we wanted an independent and noncommunist South Vietnam, which we did not get.

LIFE: It took nearly two decades for the Army to recover from the experience in Vietnam. What are your thoughts on how the Army will recover from the latest wars?

MILES: I believe the Army will recover more rapidly than after Vietnam. We should recall that the rehabilitation of the Army following Vietnam was complicated by not only the challenge of transitioning to an all-volunteer force but also issues with drugs, discipline and race that developed in the immediate aftermath of Vietnam. The setting today is quite different.

LIFE: You taught several students, including me, who went on to serve in the military. What were your feelings when we left Princeton, knowing we would be sent into combat?

MILES: I had mixed feelings. On the one hand, I was gratified by your commitment to the military and your response to the "call of duty." Moreover, I had always believed that American young men and women who wore the uniform, particularly in combat, should be led by "the best and the brightest"—that is, officers such as yourself and your peers, whose education and training would ensure effective leadership.

On the other hand, given my own experience in Vietnam, I had reservations about your being involved in a conflict that had become controversial on Capitol Hill and unpopular with the public at large.

Still, I was confident that you would be able to handle it— that as a professional soldier you would be able to put it in proper perspective.

LIFE: What is the legacy of the Vietnam War?

MILES: I believe the Vietnam Syndrome is alive and well, although in its present form it is something of a hybrid with what has been called the Iraq Syndrome. When we take note of the human cost of the Vietnam War, particularly the much larger scale of casualties, it is not surprising that the Vietnam Syndrome continues to resonate.

I also think that American political institutions, especially the presidency, have not recovered from the "credibility gap" that marked the Johnson and Nixon administrations. I would also include the collapse of the bipartisan consensus that underlay the formulation of U.S. foreign policy during the period after World War II. The old saying that politics "stops at the water's edge" in the realm of foreign affairs now seems quaint.

Finally, one consequence of the all-volunteer army, itself a product of the Vietnam War, has been increased separation of the military from the mainstream of American society. The military, of course, has always had its distinctive culture and values. But the differences now seem more pronounced.

ESCALATION

ARRIVING IN VIETNAM in 1962, Larry Burrows, one of LIFE's finest and bravest, begins shooting what has been called the most consistently excellent photography from that war. Many of his pictures were shot in color, and they were searing. In the photo here, part of a 13-page story published on January 25, 1963, a South Vietnamese paratrooper threatens a Vietcong prisoner with a bayonet.

As we have just seen, the U.S. was "in it" even before the French were out, and of course our "advisers"—members of a "Military Assistance Command"—were, like most people in Indochina, in harm's way. It is a famous fact that war would never be formally declared by Washington, so in employing another euphemism, the question, as the 1960s dawned, was how deeply would America get involved in this "conflict"? The answer: deeply indeed, with fatal consequences for millions of people, the majority of them innocent noncombatants. What was called in North Vietnam the "War Against the Americans to Save the Nation" claimed as many as a quarter million U.S. and South Vietnamese military personnel, some 1.1 million North Vietnamese and Vietcong fighters—and a stunning 2 million civilians.

The escalation progressed through the administrations of three U.S. Presidents: Kennedy, Johnson and Nixon. After the French were defeated at Dien Bien Phu in 1954, the prospect of elections to reunite Vietnam as a whole scared the West because of a likely communist win. The U.S. backed Ngo Dinh Diem's refusal to allow such a vote in the south. By decade's end, Diem had proved ineffective in curtailing the actions of the communist South Vietnamese guerrillas, the Vietcong. And when there was a major insurgency by the Vietminh, the Second Indochina War was on in earnest if not in name.

Diem in no way commanded the respect and loyalty of his people that Ho Chi Minh did in the North, and by 1963 his administration was in such a shambles that he was overthrown and assassinated by members of his own military—acting with the quiet support of the Kennedy White House. This occurred three weeks before the assassination of JFK himself in Dallas, and President Lyndon Baines Johnson inherited a confusing war being run in concert with brand-new partners in Saigon. With affairs on the ground not going well, Johnson, by late 1964, came to believe that a ramp-up of U.S. military might was the best (perhaps only) road to success, not least because the government, post-Diem, remained highly unstable and the South Vietnamese fighting force was generally ineffective.

Among new initiatives, the U.S. military began backing covert South Vietnamese raids of the North Vietnam coast. Our Navy stationed two destroyers, the *Maddox* and the *Turner Joy,* in the Gulf of Tonkin to support these operations. On August 2, attacks by North Vietnamese patrol boats on the *Maddox* were reported. Two days later, a second, now highly disputed round of attacks on the ships was reported. Johnson asked Congress for the authority to "take all necessary measures" to repel attacks against U.S. forces. The Gulf of Tonkin Resolution, not *quite* a declaration of war, passed with two dissenting votes in the Senate and none in the House and would provide the legal underpinning for all future U.S. escalation—indeed, for the American prosecution of what was clearly, all euphemisms aside, a war.

PRESIDENT KENNEDY VISITS Eglin Air Force Base in Florida on May 4, 1962, to watch a manned weapons firepower demonstration. Here, from his motorcade, he reviews the First Air Commando Group, which is trained for guerrilla warfare. The same month, Defense Secretary Robert McNamara goes to South Vietnam and reports that "we are winning the war."

AP

A U.S. ARMY HELICOPTER flies over a Catholic church in Hué, a city of 140,000 people in central Vietnam, on August 21, 1962, the jungle visible in the distance. Six years later, Hué would be a major battleground for 25 days in the North Vietnamese–initiated Tet Offensive and would be left largely in ruins.

HORST FAAS/AP

"IN INTERROGATING PRISONERS
each side in the Vietnam war occasionally
resorts to terror," Larry Burrows wrote
in a 1963 LIFE cover story titled "We Wade
Deeper Into Jungle War." Two of his
shots from that assignment are shown in
color here (left and opposite). Above: A
South Vietnamese soldier cocks a pistol as he
questions two Vietcong guerrillas, hands
bound, who have been captured in a marsh.
Far left: A child on the back of his uniformed
father is treated by a U.S. medic.

HORST FAAS/AP (2)

LARRY BURROWS © LARRY BURROWS COLLECTION

UNLIKE PREVIOUS WARS
America had fought, there was no "front" in Vietnam. The enemy could appear anywhere, and battles were waged in the water and in the air as well as on the ground. Opposite: South Vietnamese soldiers travel the Mekong Delta in a canoe-like boat looking for Vietcong. Right: Paratroopers of the 6th Vietnamese airborne battalion drift earthward northeast of Saigon in an operation against the communist guerrillas.

MICHAEL RENARD/AP

"THE DRAGON LADY," she was called. Beautiful and glamorous, South Vietnamese de facto first lady Madame Nhu could also be heartless, as when she callously dismissed the Buddhist monk who burned himself to death in protest against her brother-in-law's brutal regime (please see page 63). "I would clap hands at another monk barbecue show," she wrote in a letter to *The New York Times*, "for one cannot be responsible for the madness of others." Below, she stands with her husband, President Diem's brother, and plays with her two-year-old daughter. Right: In a photo for the October 26, 1962, issue of LIFE, she aims a .38 pistol as women in military uniforms look on.

LARRY BURROWS © LARRY BURROWS COLLECTION

LARRY BURROWS/LIFE (2)

HENRY CABOT LODGE, appointed ambassador to South Vietnam by President Kennedy in 1963, quickly becomes frustrated with Diem's government. (The two are shown together at left.) One reason: "the Buddhist crisis." To protest the oppression of Buddhists by Diem, a Catholic, monks demonstrate in the streets of Saigon in the spring and summer, culminating in a horrific event that is captured on film (opposite) by AP correspondent Malcolm Wilde Browne. In the early morning of June 11, an elderly monk, Thich Quang Duc, sits down at a busy intersection and fellow monks douse him with gasoline. Moments later, the monk, seated lotus style, lights a match and sets himself on fire, meditating as he burns to death. The whole world is suddenly watching events that are unfolding in Vietnam.

LARRY BURROWS/LIFE

MALCOLM BROWNE/AP (2)

COMFORT AMID CARNAGE:
A South Vietnamese Marine, severely wounded in a Vietcong ambush, is held by a comrade in a sugar cane field at Duc Hoa, about 12 miles from Saigon, in August 1963. A platoon of 30 Marines had been searching for communist guerrillas when a long burst of automatic fire killed one Marine and wounded four others. The war, from an American perspective, is no longer theoretical.

THE BUDDHIST CRISIS

eventually leads to the demise of the Diem regime. Shortly after the monk's self-immolation in Saigon, South Vietnamese military officers ask the United States how it would respond to a military uprising. President Kennedy is at first noncommittal but then in August 1963 sends a cable to Lodge that many believe sets the course for the bloody coup that occurs on November 1, when South Vietnamese generals storm the palace. Diem and his brother had escaped beforehand and were promised safe exile if they surrendered. Instead, they are shot to death in the back of an armored personnel carrier. One historian later calls the missive from Kennedy "the single most controversial cable of the Vietnam War"—which is really saying something. On these pages: Rebel troops and Vietnamese civilians at the gates of the Presidential Palace on November 5.

"MCNAMARA'S WAR" is what Vietnam came to be called. In his book *The Best and the Brightest,* David Halberstam describes the U.S. defense secretary as "the can-do man in the can-do society in the can-do era," and indeed, with his steely mind and boundless confidence, Robert McNamara was seen as President Johnson's smartest cabinet member—and a hawk who bore a large responsibility for America's growing involvement in the war. In March 1964, he visits South Vietnam (opposite, top) and declares that its new leader, General Nguyen Khanh (left of McNamara, who is in the middle), "has our admiration, our respect and our complete support," adding: "We'll stay for as long as it takes. We shall provide whatever help is required to win the battle against the communist insurgents." Although his enthusiasm for the war makes him a target for blistering criticism at home, he does have his supporters in Vietnam (opposite, bottom). For 20 years after the war's end, McNamara stays silent on his role in the conflict, but then in 1995 he issues an apology in his memoir, titled *In Retrospect:* "We were wrong, terribly wrong," he writes. "We owe it to future generations to explain why." Left: Dennis Driscoll, the nine-year-old son of Lieutenant Colonel Arthur Driscoll, guards his front door following Vietcong terrorist bombings in Saigon in March 1964.

STARK SCENES from May 1964, in a rapidly escalating war (clockwise from left): Captured Vietcong guerrillas being taken by helicopter for questioning; Vietnamese soldiers with a Vietcong suspect near the Cambodian border; houses set on fire by Vietnamese infantry in a "shoot on sight" area near the Cambodian border where peasants have been moved out; Vietnamese soldiers escorting Vietcong guerrilla suspects from a "cleared" village; and a Vietnamese officer with civilians who have attempted to return to their village against orders.

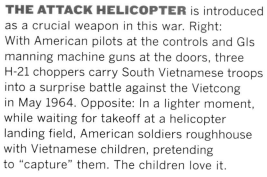

THE ATTACK HELICOPTER is introduced as a crucial weapon in this war. Right: With American pilots at the controls and GIs manning machine guns at the doors, three H-21 choppers carry South Vietnamese troops into a surprise battle against the Vietcong in May 1964. Opposite: In a lighter moment, while waiting for takeoff at a helicopter landing field, American soldiers roughhouse with Vietnamese children, pretending to "capture" them. The children love it.

LARRY BURROWS © LARRY BURROWS COLLECTION

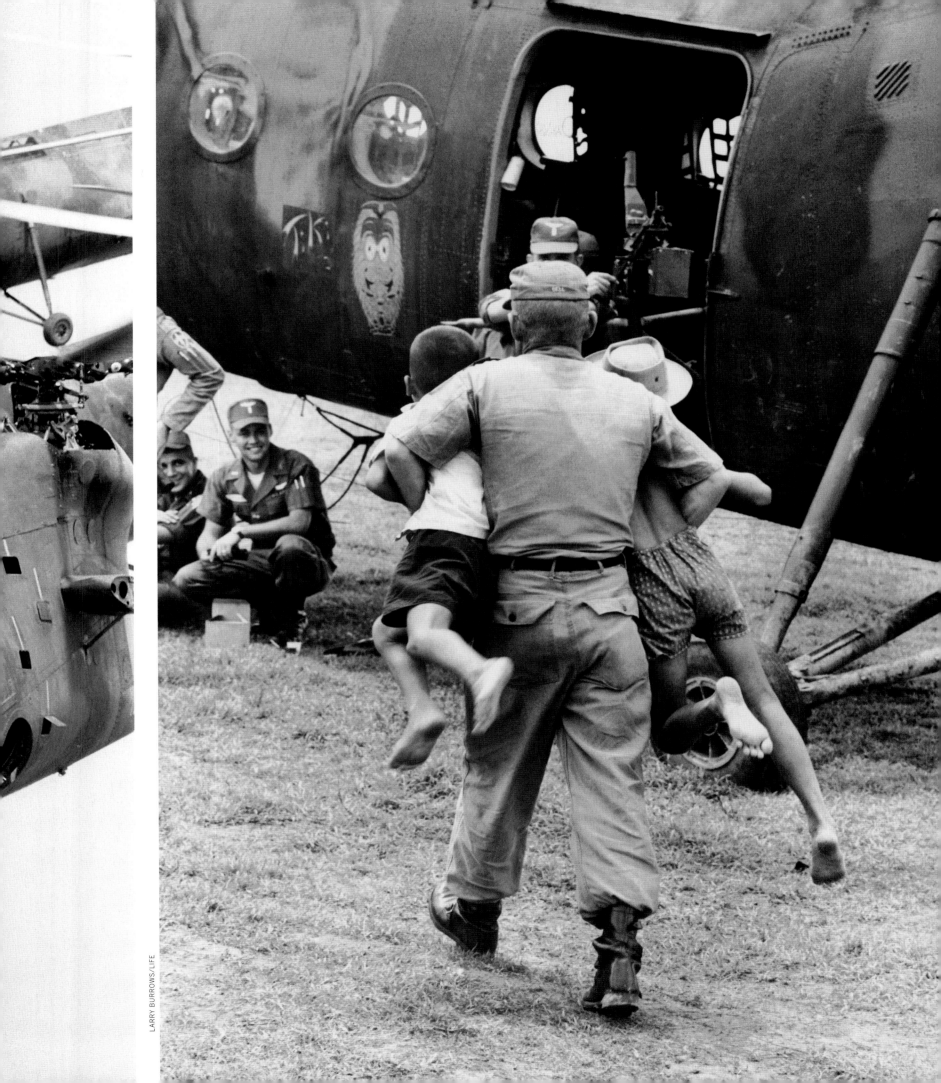

OUTRAGE IS SPREADING in the United States as well as in Asia. Top left: Vietnamese troops with fixed bayonets face protesters in Saigon in August 1964. Left: The same month, a demonstrator clutches his glasses as New York City police officers subdue him in Times Square. Opposite: A New York City police officer escorts a woman carrying a paper bag and a torn placard—one of 250 demonstrators who have attempted to hold a rally in Duffy Square and are being battled by police. When the protesters attempt to walk toward the United Nations headquarters about 30 arrests are made.

AP (3)

LARRY BURROWS/LIFE

LARRY BURROWS © LARRY BURROWS COLLECTION (2)

IN A PHOTO ESSAY ABOUT THE WORSENING CRISIS in the November 27, 1964, issue of LIFE, U.S. Army Special Forces Captain Vernon Gillespie Jr. searches for Vietcong. Top: Gillespie radios base camp while South Vietnamese soldiers burn down a suspected Vietcong hideout. Above, left: Gillespie plays with local children. Above, right: American children of servicemen stationed in Saigon are guarded as they attend school. Opposite: Bob Hope arrives for his first annual Christmas show in Vietnam, a tradition he would continue through 1972. With Anita Bryant and Jill St. John accompanying him that first year, he swung his golf club and cracked jokes, and when he got home he told reporters, "That was the most exciting Christmas show since 1943."

AP

ONE RIDE WITH
YANKEE PAPA 13

IN THE HEART OF THE HORROR, Lance Corporal James C. Farley, helicopter crew chief, yells to his pilot after a firefight outside Da Nang, a coastal city in central Vietnam that in 1965 is serving the South Vietnamese effort as one of the busiest air bases in the war.

Honored as perhaps "the greatest photo essay ever made," this was the masterpiece in the career of Larry Burrows, who was called by LIFE managing editor Ralph Graves "the single bravest and most dedicated war photographer I know of." We have already heard of Burrows in our introduction to this book and seen some of his early photographs from Vietnam; we will revisit many more of them—and his continuing story—in the pages to follow. Regarding this piece, which ran in LIFE on April 16, 1965: *Yankee Papa 13* was the name of a Marine helicopter whose crew, a squadron of U.S. Marines, was given the job of ferrying a battalion of Vietnamese infantry to an isolated area 20 miles away. That area was a rendezvous point for enemy Vietcong forces. The day began like any other day, but by the end disaster had laid its cruel hand on several very young men. In turn, this photo essay, once published back home, sounded a clarion call to a naïve America that serious trouble was brewing in a faraway land.

Thirty-five hundred American Marines, the first American combat troops, had arrived in Vietnam in March 1965, and that was a story that needed documenting—a task Burrows always accomplished with a camera. He was looking at the widening war generally, but the events of a chaotic helicopter mission on March 31, "Yankee Papa," as the story has come to be known, yielded a focused piece that spoke to larger happenings. Burrows, LIFE's editors wrote at the time, "had been covering the war in Vietnam since 1962 and had flown on scores of helicopter missions. On this day he would be riding in [21-year-old crew chief James] Farley's machine—and both were wondering whether the mission would be a no-contact milk run or whether, as had been increasingly the case in recent weeks, the Vietcong would be ready and waiting with .30-caliber machine guns. In a very few minutes Farley and Burrows had their answer."

Burrows remembered: "The Vietcong, dug in along the tree line, were just waiting for us to come into the landing zone. We were all like sitting ducks and their raking crossfire was murderous. Over the intercom system one pilot radioed Lieutenant Colonel Norman G. Ewers, who was in the lead ship: 'Colonel, We're being hit.' Back came the reply: 'We're all being hit. If your plane is flyable, press on.'"

WITH A FATEFUL MISSION SOON TO BEGIN, the men who are about to board *Yankee Papa 13* and other helicopters are attentive yet relaxed as they receive instructions.

PREPARING FOR ACTION, opposite, is LIFE's Burrows, mounting a camera onto a special rig attached to an M-60 machine gun that will be aboard helicopter *YP13*—known fully if less formally as *Yankee Papa 13*. At right is a seemingly carefree young warrior, Lance Corporal James C. Farley, toting two more M-60s to the helicopter. There are concerns about their near future at this point, certainly, but the worries aren't great and are nowhere evident in these photographs. *Yankee Papa 13* is one of a squadron of 17 choppers transporting South Vietnamese troops near Da Nang at the time. As for Farley, the son of an Army master sergeant who fought in World War II, he joined the Marines right after graduating from high school in Tucson, Arizona, because, as he would tell *People* magazine two decades after these photos were made, "they were supposed to be the toughest and the baddest. I was a 98-pound weakling who wanted to prove something to the world." In early 1965, upon arriving in Vietnam, he figured he was entering "a tiny little fight." Before and after the dramatic "Yankee Papa" mission recorded by Burrows, he knew better: "The war was getting to be a joke. The generals weren't calling the shots. I couldn't see myself as anything other than a target."

PRESENT REALITY is made clear as *Yankee Papa 13* swoops in. Opposite, top: Farley adjusts his helmet. Below: A camera Burrows has mounted outside the helicopter shows Farley firing his M-60 on the approach to the landing zone. Right, top: South Vietnamese soldiers scramble out of the chopper to join in the assault against Vietcong forces hidden along the tree line in the background. Right: Men from airworthy helicopters concentrate on helping those from disabled aircraft. *Yankee Papa 13* presses on, as instructed by Lieutenant Colonel Ewers. Remembered Burrows, in words transcribed for the LIFE article from an audio recording made shortly after the mission, he, Farley and the others hurried "back to a pickup point for another load of troops. On our next approach to the landing zone, our pilot, Captain Peter Vogel, spotted *Yankee Papa 3* down on the ground. Its engine was still on and the rotors turning, but the ship was obviously in trouble. 'Why don't they lift off?' Vogel muttered over the intercom. Then he set down our ship nearby to see what the trouble was." That investigation would have distressing results.

FARLEY HAS CLIMBED

onto the mysteriously immobile *Yankee Papa 3* in an attempt to see what he could do for the pilot. But upon seeing that the man has been shot in the neck, Farley assumes he is dead and runs from *YP3* back to his own chopper (note that Burrows, at this moment, must be unsheltered as well, and in the path of gunfire). In the photograph opposite and in the one that opens this story, there is more chaos once Farley returns to *Yankee Papa 13*. His rescue mission botched, he heads back to base with the dead and wounded and discovers that his machine gun is now jammed (please see page 78). *Yankee Papa 13* has 11 bullet holes in its skin and its radio is knocked out. "The Plexiglas had been shot out of the cockpit and one Vietcong bullet had nicked our pilot's neck," reported Burrows. "Our radio and instruments were out of commission. We climbed and climbed fast the hell out of there." After *Yankee Papa 13* limps back to base, the civilian Burrows is given a set of air crewman's wings by squadron chief Lieutenant Colonel Ewers, who says succinctly, "You've earned it."

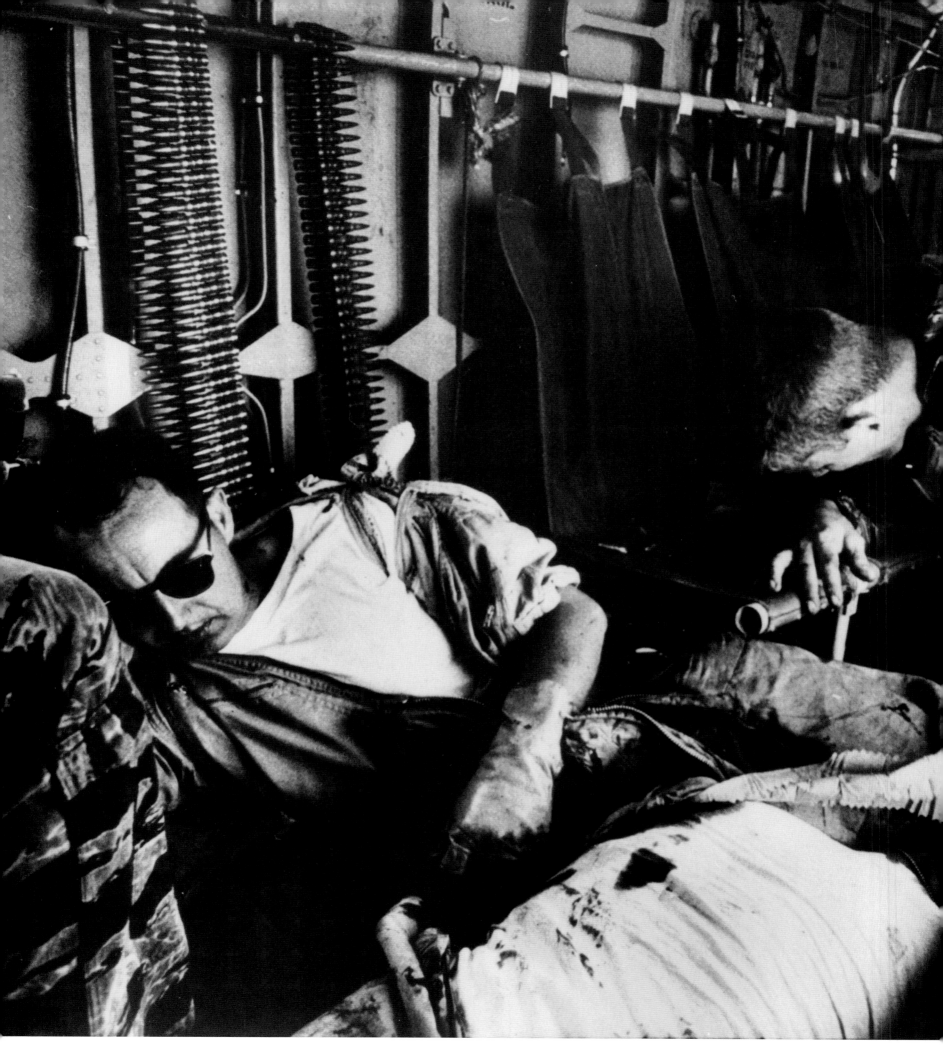

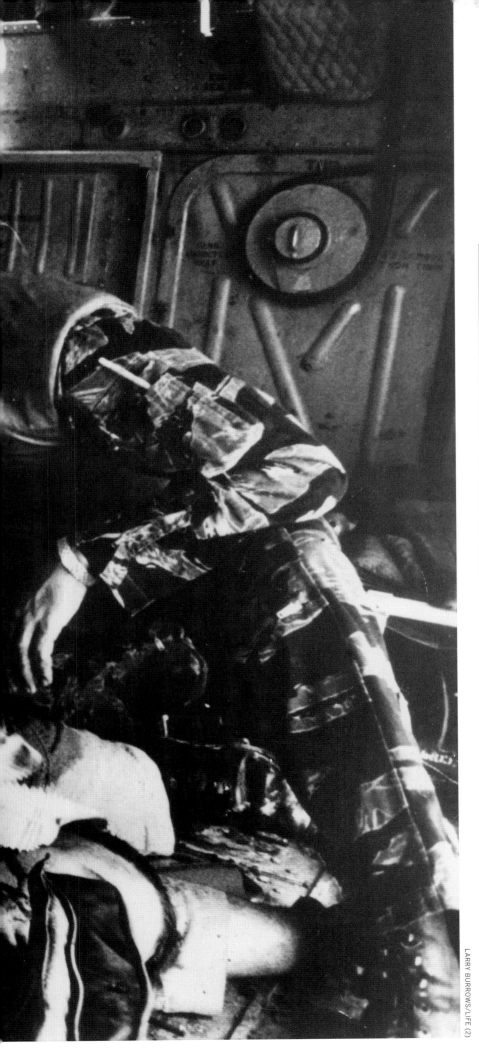

LARRY BURROWS/LIFE (2)

SERGEANT BILLIE OWENS, badly wounded in the shoulder, leans against Private First Class Wayne Hoilien while Farley attends to both men on the last leg of the journey home (left). Back at the base, Farley talks to his weary men, reports in, then, retreating to the privacy of a supply shack, yields to the day (above). "When I got back from Vietnam I was very proud," the man who flew another eight months after this mission will say 20 years after the ordeal. "But after a while I wouldn't talk about my experiences. It would almost always guarantee a fight." He was unable to shake the memories or visceral sensations of his experience: "I can smell blood from far away. In Vietnam you learned to recognize it. I used to hose down the helicopter after it had been filled with blood."

QUAGMIRE

SHELL SHOCKED: This photograph of a U.S. Marine could be used as a definition of that phrase. Taken in 1966, it shows a young man getting his wounds bandaged in a muddy jungle during Operation Prairie, an American military sweep of the area just south of the Demilitarized Zone, the dividing line between North and South Vietnam. The Marines famously fight on water, on land—anywhere—and are often the first ones in. As was the case in Vietnam.

HORST FAAS/AP

When he succeeded John Fitzgerald Kennedy as President of the United States, Lyndon Baines Johnson had wanted to focus on domestic matters—civil rights legislation, the building of his Great Society—and yet he bothered to say very quickly, "the battle against communism . . . must be joined . . . with strength and determination." While strength could be summoned by decree in Washington, determination would erode over time—throughout the nation and finally in the halls of Congress and even in the military ranks. Was this a winnable war? More important, and more frequently asked as time went on: Was it in any way a *just* war?

In the weeks before he was killed, Kennedy wrestled with the future of the U.S.'s military and economic support to Vietnam. Whether he would have increased American involvement or initiated a withdrawal of personnel is still sharply debated. Johnson, for his part, campaigned in the 1964 election on the promise that he would not escalate the war, declaring he was not keen to commit "American boys to fighting a war that I think ought to be fought by the boys of Asia to help protect their own land." But frustrations mounted over South Vietnamese ineptitude (military and also political), and Johnson, after the election, began to waver. He was certainly aware that the communists, though losing greater numbers than the South Vietnamese in the field, were growing more formidable. In the five years following 1959, the Vietcong fighting force had grown from 5,000 to 100,000, and in that period more than 7,000 South Vietnamese villages had been destroyed. The North Vietnamese army now numbered nearly a million; the math was portentous. Ho Chi Minh reiterated what he had told the French much earlier: If Americans "want to make war for 20 years, then we shall make war for 20 years. If they want to make peace, we shall make peace and invite them to afternoon tea."

Peace not being seen as an option, the U.S. Marines arrived in big numbers and with this commitment came some successes. A turning point, in several ways, was the Tet Offensive of January 1968. In that instance, the communists sought to surprise their foes by breaking the traditional truce enforced during Tet, the lunar new year celebration. With 70,000 troops, they attacked more than 100 cities and towns, including Saigon. American and South Vietnamese forces largely repelled the attacks, though an estimated 3,000 people were killed in the city of Hué, which was virtually destroyed.

Back home in the U.S., the effects of this huge offensive and its aftermath could be quickly gauged in the public perception of General William Westmoreland, who was prosecuting the war for our side. *Time* magazine had named him its Man of the Year in 1965—"the sinewy personification of the American fighting man . . . [the man who oversaw] the historic buildup, drew up the battle plans, and infused the . . . men under him with his own idealistic view of U.S. aims and responsibilities." Now he was on the magazine's cover again, his stock plummeting. Within weeks of the Tet Offensive, polls showed that those who thought the United States was making progress in the war had plunged from 51 to 32 percent. And for the first time, a majority—just over 50 percent—thought it had been a mistake to send U.S. troops to Vietnam.

Washington's response as the spirit sagged in the later 1960s was to, as Air Force Chief of Staff General Curtis LeMay put it, "bomb them back into the Stone Age." From 1965 to late 1968, operation Rolling Thunder besieged North Vietnam with a million tons of missiles, rockets and bombs. In places, the smell of napalm greeted many each morning.

But Ho Chi Minh had not been wrong. If it would take 20 years, it would take 20 years. Worldwide, this boast came to be regarded as fact. The United States was exactly where the French had been, and it would soon need to find a way out.

THE VIETNAM WAR put U.S. soldiers in frequent contact with civilians—and killed 2 million of them. Here, on New Year's Day 1966, an American paratrooper holds an M79 grenade launcher as two South Vietnamese children and their mothers huddle against a canal bank for protection from Vietcong sniper fire.

STUDENTS FOR A DEMOCRATIC SOCIETY thought that just a small crowd would rally at their April 17, 1965, March on Washington to End the War in Vietnam. Instead, an estimated 25,000 converged in the capital, making it the largest antiwar protest so far. "It is time we showed President Johnson and the Congress that thousands of Americans decry our dangerous and immoral policy in Vietnam," read a flyer encouraging people to attend the demonstration. "This is an action for the entire family. Husbands and children must march with us. Bring friends, relatives, bring grandchildren, neighbors. Come by car, come by bus, come by train." And they did.

PHOTOGRAPH © DANIEL KRAMER

THE FIRST U.S. COMBAT TROOPS land in Vietnam in 1965, and LIFE photographer Paul Schutzer accompanies U.S. Marines during a conflict near the North-South border and takes the photos on this page and on the opposite page, top, for the November 26 issue. The photo at far right, of a Vietcong prisoner with his mouth and eyes taped for security, runs on the cover and is seen as controversial. In the bottom photograph on the opposite page, Marines recover the body of a comrade while under fire. The French-born Catherine Leroy, one of the few female war photographers in Indochina at this time, appears in the background. Above that is a picture by Schutzer of a Marine carrying an injured Vietnamese child.

LARRY BURROWS/LIFE

PAUL SCHUTZER/LIFE (5)

HIROJI KUBOTA/MAGNUM

AP

ANDREW SCHNEIDER/THREE LIONS/GETTY

MARC RIBOUD/MAGNUM

"BEARDS AND BLUE JEANS mixed with Ivy tweeds and an occasional clerical collar in the crowd," *The New York Times* reports about the April 1965 March on Washington, in reference to the mix of students, faculty members and clergy in the crowd. Joan Baez (opposite) is among the folk singers who perform protest songs. Elsewhere around the country, young men burn their draft cards, which is illegal but happens in demonstrations in numerous cities (top left, in New York City). Top right: Protesters march against the war in Berkeley, California. Above, left: Members of the National Mobilization Committee to End the War in Vietnam (known as MOBE and for its motto, "What are we waiting for?") are on the move during a 1965 protest. Above, right: The counterculture confronts the establishment in the March on the Pentagon in October 1967, which draws 100,000 people. Dr. Benjamin Spock (who had given child-rearing advice to the parents of so many of these kids), Abbie Hoffman and Norman Mailer are in attendance, and Mailer later chronicles the events in his Pulitzer Prize–winning book *The Armies of the Night*.

AP

"YOU JUST TAKE GASOLINE, sprinkle in some powder, and stir." That's the recipe for napalm, the jellylike substance that causes severe burns on contact, as provided by Harvard chemist Louis Fieser, who invented it in the 1940s. He said he never dreamed it would be used on people, only things. But when its employment is authorized by President Johnson in March 1965, it becomes a terrifying weapon in the Vietnam War. Opposite: In 1966, an American jet drops napalm and phosphorous bombs on a small village known to be a Vietcong stronghold. Above: A napalm strike erupts in a fireball near U.S. troops on patrol in South Vietnam, also in 1966. Right: The crew of an American gunship firing during a night mission, as photographed by Larry Burrows. The war's most infamous napalm photo appears on page 146.

LARRY BURROWS/LIFE

LARRY BURROWS © LARRY BURROWS COLLECTION

"THE HILL OF ANGELS," the Vietnamese called it. The U.S. Marine outpost at Con Thien was a small hill, about 520 feet high and two miles south of the DMZ, affording a prominent view of activity in the area. Strategically important because it was situated along the so-called McNamara Line, intended to prevent the North Vietnamese Army from making its way into South Vietnam, the Hill of Angels saw intense and bloody fighting in the late '60s. On these pages, David Douglas Duncan captures Marines under fire during a battle there in a famous image that also appears on our book's cover. "I always used to go on my own," Duncan says today from his home in the south of France. "I had been a Marine; I went in alone. That's why there aren't a lot of other pictures from Con Thien."

HAUNTED AND HAUNTING: Larry Burrows captures a look of fear on a soldier's face in 1966 (right). Above are two pictures by LIFE's Co Rentmeester: American soldiers using rope to help a recovery vehicle pull a stuck M48 tank out of the mud on Route 13, which links Vietnam to the Cambodian border (top), and a makeshift memorial erected to fallen comrades in the aftermath of the Battle of Dak To in November 1967.

CO RENTMEESTER/LIFE (2)

LARRY BURROWS/LIFE

"**HE HAD BEEN THROUGH SO MUCH,** always coming out magically unscathed, that a myth of invulnerability grew up about him," LIFE managing editor Ralph Graves wrote in the February 19, 1971, issue, when the photograph on these pages was first published, five years after Larry Burrows shot it. "Friends came to believe he was protected by some invisible armor. But I don't think he believed that himself. Whenever he went in harm's way he knew, precisely, what the dangers were and how vulnerable he was." The picture, which has come to be called "Reaching Out," shows one wounded Marine, Gunnery Sergeant Jeremiah Purdie, approaching another in a gesture of human kindness amid horror and became one of the war's most memorable images. It was not published when made in October 1966 during a helicopter evacuation of Mutter Ridge, Nui Cay Tri, but only much later, having been discovered in Burrows's slide tray after a helicopter carrying him and three other photojournalists was shot down over Laos. Purdie, wounded here for the third time in Vietnam, lived, and is seen again in our book on page 153.

THE BATTLE OF KHE SANH has been called the longest and deadliest of the war. Accounts differ as to the number of casualties and what the battle meant to the larger conflict, but there is no question that its 77 days of hellish combat in 1968 were pivotal. "American forces rained 100,000 tons of bombs (equivalent in destructive force to five Hiroshima-size atomic bombs) and 158,000 large-caliber shells on the hills surrounding the base, killing an estimated 15,000 Communist soldiers," *The New York Times* later reported. For the U.S. troops, "there is no feeling in the world as good as being airborne out of Khe Sanh," journalist Michael Herr wrote about the battle that serves as the centerpiece of his 1977 book, *Dispatches*. Here, a helicopter delivers ammunition and supplies to U.S. Marines on one of those hellish 77 days.

LARRY BURROWS/LIFE

THE EXECUTION OF ONE VIETCONG GUERRILLA

"would hardly have seemed especially noteworthy in a week when women and children were beheaded in Saigon," reported *The New York Times*. But when South Vietnamese General Nguyen Ngoc Loan, chief of the national police, pointed his pistol and shot Nguyen Van Lem on February 1, 1968, AP photographer Eddie Adams captured the moment: the prisoner with his hands tied behind his back, Loan appearing calm as he shot Lem from point-blank range, Lem's final grimace as the bullet passed through his head. The picture, which won the Pulitzer Prize in 1969, was viewed around the world as a symbol of savagery and turned American sentiment further against the war, but Loan insisted his act was justified because Lem had murdered the family of one of his soldiers. He also countered the opinion that the shooting had been impulsive. Rather, he explained, he did the job because a deputy commander who had been ordered to do so had hesitated. "I think, *Then I must do it,*" Loan recalled. "If you hesitate, if you didn't do your duty, the men won't follow you." Adams, knowing that the photo ruined Loan's life, later said he regretted the anguish his picture caused: "The general killed the Vietcong; I killed the general with my camera." When Loan died in 1998, leaving a wife and five children, Adams sent flowers with a card that read, "I'm sorry. There are tears in my eyes."

EDDIE ADAMS/AP

ART GREENSPAN/AP

AP

JOHN OLSON/THE LIFE IMAGES COLLECTION/GETTY

PHILIP JONES GRIFFITHS/MAGNUM

SOME OF THE MOST HEARTBREAKING PICTURES coming out of Vietnam were those depicting the wounded, often being cared for by their comrades. Opposite: A medical corpsman holds the head of an injured Marine, William Michael "Mike" Welch, talking quietly to calm him. This page, clockwise from top left: A paratrooper guides a medical evacuation helicopter through the jungle to pick up casualties as fellow troopers aid their wounded buddies; a medic looks up at a helicopter while treating an injured soldier; a young girl, killed by U.S. helicopter fire during the Tet Offensive, lays in the back of a truck, where her distraught brother found her; wounded troops ride in a tank used as a makeshift ambulance after a battle.

THE MY LAI MASSACRE was far from the only atrocity committed by troops, on all sides, in Vietnam. But it is the one that became and has remained synonymous with the rape, torture and murder of innocent civilians during war—and synonymous with American shame. The facts are these: On March 16, 1968, more than 20 members of Charlie Company, the U.S. Army's 1st Battalion 20th Infantry, having been sent on a search-and-destroy mission to find Vietcong, arrive in the tiny village and, despite encountering no resistance, slaughter hundreds of people (estimates vary from 347 to 507), mostly women, children and old men. Army photographer Ron Haeberle was there that day and shot the photos on these pages, waiting more than a year before sharing them with his hometown newspaper, the Cleveland *Plain Dealer,* and then with LIFE, which published them in the December 5, 1969, issue. After the ensuing investigation and court-martial, one man, Lieutenant William Calley Jr. (this page, top left), was found guilty of the premeditated murder of at least 22 Vietnamese civilians. He served three years under house arrest and was released on parole in 1974. In 2009 he apologized.

WEARY AFTER YEARS OF WAR, President Johnson works on a speech in the White House Cabinet Room on March 30, 1968, the day before shocking the nation with his announcement that he wouldn't run for reelection. "I shall not seek, and I will not accept, the nomination of my party for another term as your President," he says during his televised address about the Vietnam War, citing politics as the reason for his decision. "There is division in the American house now. There is divisiveness among us all tonight," he says. "With America's sons in the fields far away, with America's future under challenge right here at home, with our hopes and the world's hopes for peace in the balance every day, I do not believe that I should devote an hour or a day of my time to any personal partisan causes." Many believe, however, that the embattled President has withdrawn because he fears he will lose the election.

THE SIEGE
OF CHICAGO

"A YEAR OF VIOLENCE, war and heartbreak in the nation [coming] to a head in the city heat" is how Chicago History Museum curator Jill Thomas Austin described the turmoil at the 1968 Democratic National Convention. Opposite: Activists protest the detention of Tom Hayden, one of the principal organizers of the demonstrations, in Grant Park.

By the summer of 1968, the U.S. involvement in Vietnam had become the nation's flash-point political issue, and protests against the war were regular occurrences. Now came the presidential election cycle, and not only individual candidates but the Republican and Democratic conventions would be targets. Certainly, there were demonstrations during the first week in August outside the Miami Beach Convention Center as Republicans convened and nominated Richard M. Nixon on the first ballot. But the Democratic gathering, to be held from August 26 to 29 in Chicago, promised to be more problematic by half because the argument was up for grabs. The Republicans were perceived to be hawkish on Vietnam. The Democratic debate had for months been contentious: LBJ initially defiant and then withdrawing from the race; Vice President Hubert Humphrey bearing the standard forward; Senator Eugene McCarthy of Minnesota making headway with an insurgent antiwar candidacy; Robert Kennedy following McCarthy into the fray and rising, then being assassinated. In the lead-up to the last week in August, Mayor Richard J. Daley of Chicago promised to put down demonstrations and vowed, "Law and order will be maintained."

Activists, soon to be demonstrators—David Dellinger, Rennie Davis, Tom Hayden leading them—had begun planning their protests as early as March at a camp in Lake Villa, Illinois. It is said that 100 or more antiwar groups were "in." Jerry Rubin and Abbie Hoffman said their Youth International Party would bring 100,000 to Chicago. The city denied their permit for a Yippie Festival, which dissuaded the prospective protesters not at all.

The year had already been violent and awful. Columbia University had been shut down. Martin Luther King had been killed and riots had followed everywhere. Andy Warhol had been shot. RFK had been killed. President Johnson was approved of by barely a third of his country, and his Vietnam War had less than 25 percent support.

Inside the convention hall, the fight was brutal, with Humphrey, the presumptive (and eventual) nominee finally committing himself to Johnson Administration policies vis-à-vis Vietnam. Outside on the streets, the situation was much worse still. Nearly 12,000 Chicago police and 6,000 Illinois National Guardsmen countered demonstrators for five full days beginning on August 25. The so-called Battle of Michigan Avenue saw protesters fiercely stopped with tear gas from marching to the convention hall. The chant "The whole world is watching" reverberated throughout . . . well, the whole world.

Chicago police arrested nearly 600 protesters; at least 150 of the police ranks and more than 100 demonstrators were injured. There would be a famous trial in Chicago. The short of it is: Richard Nixon was elected President by a hair's breadth, and what role the siege of Chicago played is debated still.

"IF YOU'RE COMING to Chicago, be sure to wear some armor in your hair," advised the *Chicago Seed,* an alternative weekly newspaper. Left: Police officers amassed by Mayor Daley confront tens of thousands of protesters outside the Chicago Hilton.

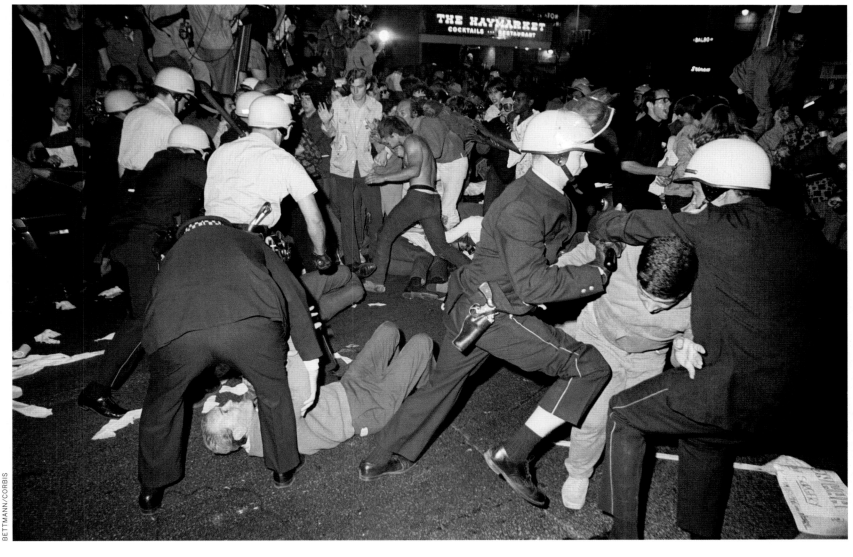

NEW YORK DAILY NEWS ARCHIVE/GETTY

BETTMANN/CORBIS

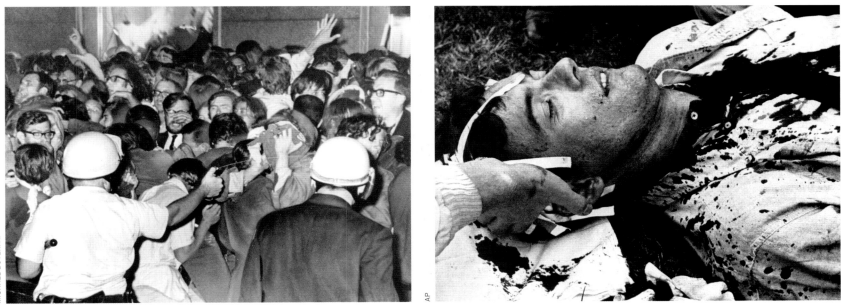

MICHAEL BOYER/AP

AP

GERALD BRIMACOMBE

PAINTING A PICTURE of the scene outside the Hilton in the September 6, 1968, issue of LIFE, Paul O'Neil wrote: "The cops attacked. New companies advanced at a half trot up a side street, fired tear gas and plunged—amid screams—into the crowds. They clubbed madly at the heads of their tormenters, beat them on the pavement, dragged them, bloody, by the dozen to a waiting paddy wagon. They chased them down sidewalks. They chased them, clubs thudding, into the hotel itself." Opposite, top: Youth scuffling. Bottom: National Guard seal the Hilton. This page: The melee (top); a police officer squirting mace (above, left); an injured protester in Grant Park (above, right).

PERRY C. RIDDLE/SUN-TIMES MEDIA

JACK THORNELL/AP

A FURIOUS MAYOR DALEY seethes on August 28 (left) as he hears convention speakers denounce his police force's extreme reaction to the unrest in the streets (above). Daley, who privately opposed the war, was vilified at the gathering. "Is there a law by which Mayor Daley can be compelled to suspend police state terror?" Colorado delegate Bob Maytag asked on the convention floor. In a speech in support of George McGovern, who had offered himself as a stand-in for the slain Robert Kennedy, U.S. senator from Connecticut Abraham Ribicoff declared: "With George McGovern as President of the United States, we wouldn't have Gestapo tactics on the streets of Chicago." A report later placed most of the blame for the riots on the Chicago police. Daley disagreed and gave the police a raise. Five of the so-called Chicago 7, protesters prosecuted for their disruption of the peace, among them Tom Hayden and Abbie Hoffman, were convicted of intent to incite a riot, but the convictions were later overturned.

COMING HOME

"NO ONE SAID THANK YOU"—this was a phenomenon commonly reported by the troops returning to the United States. After the horror of Vietnam, another hell awaited them at home: "Baby killer," they heard. They were spat upon. "I flew back to my family in Maine," veteran Alan Cutter later wrote in the *Guardian.* "They were glad to see me, but not even they said, 'Welcome home' or 'Thank you.' Even if they had, I wouldn't have known how to respond." Here, in April 1967, returning vet Mike Cowenhaven hugs Mrs. Rusher, a family friend who was like a second mother to him, in Monterey, California.

President Nixon's approach to ending the war in the late 1960s and early '70s seemed to send mixed messages. In November 1969 he sought "Vietnamization," a change in American policy with the goal of having the South Vietnamese fight their own war with American support but no substantial contribution of troops; five months later he announced that by the spring of 1971 there would be achieved "a total reduction of 265,500 men in our Armed Forces in Vietnam below the level that existed when we took office 15 months ago." Meanwhile, he escalated bombing campaigns, including new ones in Cambodia, and even feinted with nuclear weapons borne by a squadron of B-52s—bombs that were never dropped. And in the midst of all that, Nixon's administration engaged in all sorts of negotiations: détente with the Soviets, cordial hellos with the Chinese ("Ping-Pong diplomacy") and, eventually, the formal peace talks in Paris. But in the midst of all *that,* he fought the fierce domestic fallout of the My Lai Massacre and other awful news from Vietnam by asking the "silent majority" to support his plan to end the war. It seemed we were winding down one day, winding up the next—probably a fitting conclusion to a conflict that had seen the U.S., in the period following World War II, hedging its bets on which side to back.

In September 1969, Ho Chi Minh died at 79. The following year, the incursions into Cambodia along its border with Vietnam led to nationwide demonstrations in the United States and four students were killed by the National Guard at Kent State University in Ohio. The White House seemed indifferent, and the bombing was ceaseless. In June 1969 the faces of 242 U.S. servicemen killed during a week of war appeared in a cover story in LIFE (a page of which appears opposite). The response was enormous, fanning the flames of increasingly large and sometimes violent protests. Walter Cronkite's earlier reports from Vietnam for the *CBS Evening News* had a similar effect. In 1971, the Pentagon Papers were leaked to *The New York Times,* and theretofore top-secret accounts of the U.S. role in Vietnam, commissioned by the Defense Department, depicted a long trail of misinformation and outright deceit. More protests still.

In that same year, '71, the fighting spread to a section of the Ho Chi Minh trail in Laos, but by now, America was looking for a way out, not in—a fact confirmed by those chaotic and successfully repulsed advances. Our allies from Australia and New Zealand exited, and our own force was further reduced to 196,700, with a deadline to remove another 45,000 troops by February 1972. Right then, the North Vietnamese Army and the Vietcong launched an Easter Offensive and gained valuable territory in northern South Vietnam, and it became evident that if America's air assault lessened at all, the war would be lost.

In October 1972, U.S. National Security Advisor Henry Kissinger reached a tentative peace agreement with Le Duc Tho of North Vietnam (just in advance, it should be noted, of the U.S. presidential election). In November, President Nixon won a second term (not to be completed, because of the Watergate scandal). The Paris Peace Accords, which called for free elections for the North and South and were largely ignored after the fact, were signed on January 27, 1973. A ceasefire was declared. The last American ground troops departed. Prisoners of war were exchanged.

Our boys (and the few of our girls) were coming home. But this was not to the hero's welcome of World War II. Nearly 3 million Vietnam veterans survived their ordeal, and many of them were met, after baggage claim, by hawks sneering at them and doves blaming them. In 1981, Mark Baker published a strong book, *Nam: The Vietnam War in the Words of the Men and Women Who Fought There,* in which he described this new dynamic: American servicemen and -women returning from a war they had obviously not won. One soldier recalled to Baker "a guy over at a table with two kids and a woman. The kids were about my age—nineteen or twenty. 'Home on leave, are you,' the guy says to me. 'Nope, just got discharged.' 'You just got back from where,' one of the kids says. 'Vietnam.' 'How do you feel about killing all of those innocent people?' the woman asks me out of nowhere."

Another veteran, also to Baker: "I went home straight from California to O'Hare Airport in Chicago. I got home about three in the morning. Everybody in the house got up and said hello. Then they all went back to sleep. At 8:30 when my father left for work, he woke me up to say, 'Listen, now that you're home, when are you going to get a job?' I packed up and left. I haven't been home since."

Vietnam veterans from America recovered, succeeded, persevered, failed, did not recover, killed themselves, drifted off. They washed out and twice ran for President. Theirs is as heartbreaking and confusing a narrative as all else connected with this war.

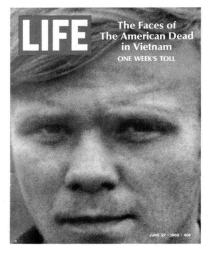

"ONE WEEK'S TOLL": LIFE's June 27, 1969, cover story (above and opposite) features photos and names of the 242 Americans killed from May 28 to June 3 of that year—10 pages devastating in their simplicity. "In a time when the numbers of Americans killed in this war—36,000—though far less than the Vietnamese losses, have exceeded the dead in the Korean War, when the nation continues week after week to be numbed by a three-digit statistic which is translated to direct anguish in hundreds of homes all over the country, we must pause to look into the faces," the accompanying text reads. "More than we must know how many, we must know who."

C. Volheim, 20
Army, SP4
yward, Calif.

Robert E. Layman, 20
Army, WO1
Poquonock, Conn.

William L. Alexander, 19
Army, SP4
Flint, Mich.

Robert J. Rosenow, 20
Army, Pfc.
La Farge, Wis.

Craig E. Yates, 18
Army, Pfc.
Sparta, Mich.

John C. Pape, 25
Army, Capt.
Amityville, N.Y.

y E. Clark, 23
Army, Pfc.
lloden, W. Va.

James P. Hickey, 19
Marines, Pfc.
West Quincy, Mass.

Mario Lamelza, 21
Army, Pfc.
Philadelphia, Pa.

Valentine Dwornik, 20
Army, SP4
Detroit, Mich.

David Tessmer, 20
Army, Pfc.
Wausau, Wis.

Gary A. Wallace, 19
Army, Pfc.
Louisville, Ky.

and Browning, 22
Army, Pfc.
Miami, Fla.

Charles C. Fleek, 21
Army, Sgt.
Petersburg, Ky.

James Patrick Francis, 22
Army, S/Sgt.
Napa, Calif.

Joe E. Bragg, 20
Army, SP4
Versailles, Ky.

William C. Gearing Jr., 20
Army, SP5
Rochester, N.Y.

Gary D. Carter, 19
Marines, Cpl.
Tyler, Texas

w T. Lozano Jr., 21
Army, Pfc.
Antonio, Texas

Winston O. Smith, 24
Army, Pfc.
Madisonville, Tenn.

Robert B. Read, 24
Army, Pfc.
Hamden, Conn.

Mark J. Haverland Jr., 21
Army, Sgt.
Poca, W. Va.

Ralph J. Mears Jr., 19
Army, SP4
Norfolk, Va.

Bruce Saunders, 21
Army, 2nd Lt.
Queens, N.Y.

KENT STATE—to this day it's all but impossible to utter those two words without evoking the four students who were killed and nine wounded on the university campus in Ohio, shot by National Guardsmen breaking up an antiwar rally on May 4, 1970. The firing started at 12:25 p.m., and 13 seconds later, Allison Krause, Sandra Scheuer, Jeffrey Miller and William Schroeder were dead. Scenes from that bloody day, counterclockwise from below: A student throws a tear gas canister back at National Guardsmen; troops aim their guns at the demonstrators; and, in the iconic photograph that earned the Pulitzer Prize for John Filo, the photojournalism student who took it, 14-year-old runaway Mary Ann Vecchio screams as she kneels next to Miller's body.

THE ANTIWAR PROTESTS reach a new level when veterans themselves band together and begin demonstrating. John Kerry, a Navy lieutenant who would become a U.S. senator and then secretary of state, marches with Vietnam Veterans Against the War (opposite, bottom) in 1971 and that same year, while testifying before the Senate Foreign Relations Committee, raises the question "How do you ask a man to be the last man to die for a mistake?" Right: Disabled veteran Ron Kovic, later played by Tom Cruise in the Oliver Stone film based on Kovic's book, *Born on the Fourth of July,* holds an upside-down flag as a symbol of distress in a 1972 protest. Amid all this, one bright spot for the nation seems to be the return of Lieutenant Colonel Robert L. Stirm, an Air Force fighter pilot who was shot down over Hanoi and held in captivity for nearly six years. Opposite, top, in a Pulitzer-winning photograph called "Burst of Joy," the POW is reunited with his family on the tarmac at Travis Air Force Base in California. But even that happy image belies sadness. Three days before, he'd received a Dear John letter from his wife (second from right); the couple would divorce shortly after his return. The four children each keep a framed copy of the photograph in their homes, but Stirm himself can't bear to display it.

LEAVING: U.S. artillerymen on the Laotian border express hope with a flag (above), and a South Vietnamese Marine carries the body of a fellow soldier killed in 1972 (left). Opposite, top: A widow cries in anguish over the remains of her husband, which were found in a mass grave. Below: Workers remove the bodies of civilians killed long before during the Tet Offensive.

TRAGEDY IN THE SKY:
Waiting for a helicopter flight
into Laos to cover Operation
Lam Son 719, a massive attack
on the Ho Chi Minh Trail
by South Vietnamese forces
on February 10, 1971, are
photojournalists (from left)
Keisaburo Shimamoto of
Newsweek, Henri Huet of AP
(with back to camera), Larry
Burrows of LIFE and Kent Potter
of UPI. The helicopter would
be shot down, killing all four.
The camaraderie and kinship
among the photographers
covering this war was so
great that 27 years later fellow
journalists returned to Southeast
Asia to look for the crash site
and the remains of their friends.
Among the found objects was
Burrows's Leica camera.

SERGIO ORTIZ

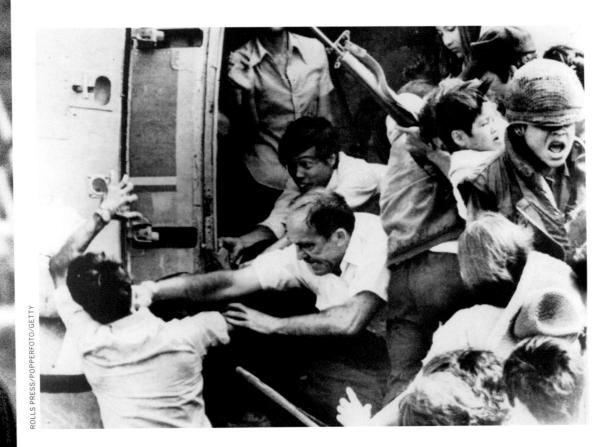

THE FALL OF SAIGON occurs, at last (left), on April 30, 1975, as North Vietnamese tanks smash through the gates of the Presidential Palace. The evacuation of Americans from the U.S. embassy is difficult as South Vietnamese, desperate to escape the advancing communist troops, shout, "We want to go too," and attempt to board the helicopters. Above: An American official punches a Vietnamese man in the face as the last chopper leaves the embassy.

THE CHILDREN
OF WAR

NGUYEN THI TRON, who was wounded in 1968 in an attack by U.S. helicopters in a forest near Saigon, is fitted for a prosthetic leg in 1969. She and two other children seen in these next few pages are presented here as emblematic of one of a tragic war's greatest of all tragedies: innocents in every sense, placed squarely in harm's way.

The Vietnam War claimed many victims from several nations who were afflicted in many and various ways. But none of the war's sad consequences were sadder than those affecting the children of Vietnam. It is uncertain how many were killed, but the most conservative estimates are at least 80,000 children under the age of 15. There were, of course, other harms done to children—many tens of thousands of injuries inflicted, 20,000 to 30,000 unwanted children born to foreign fathers who would have no regard for their well-being. The victorious Vietnamese disdained Amerasian infants in their midst, considering these babies, many of whom were left on the doorsteps of orphanages, "children of the dust." In 1970 the United States Defense Department would say, "The care and welfare of these unfortunate children . . . has never been and is not now considered an area of government responsibility." The most tenacious of these survivors did fight their way to a new life in America, although it is thought that no more than 3 percent of them were ever reunited with their fathers.

The plight of children in Vietnam was a story that western journalists eventually arrived at as the long war ground on. It has been said, not incorrectly, that LIFE photographer Larry Burrows's work became more intimate and even more compassionate in the later years of the conflict. He had thought himself a moderate hawk early on, but the more he saw of the situation in Vietnam, the more convinced he became that the story was about the victims. Two of his photo essays, known today as "Tron" and "Lau," became famous touchstones of the Vietnam War (as did AP photographer Nick Ut's shocking photograph of the child Phan Thi Kim Phúc, known as "Napalm Girl"; please see page 146).

Burrows first saw Nguyen Thi Tron when she was 12 years old in 1968. She was sitting on a swing with another child in Saigon; they had one leg between them and Tron was propelling the swing. Tron had gone into the forest to collect firewood and plants. She had innocently entered a "free-fire zone," where anyone might be expected to be Vietcong. A patrolling helicopter spotted her and opened fire. The Americans landed and, discovering their mistake, airlifted Tron to the hospital. Her mother used part of the $35 the Americans gave her to pay for her daughter's blood transfusions. Burrows took the photo on the opposite page in '68. His granddaughter, Sarah, took the photo of Tron at left in 2000, after finding her, at age 44, in the village of Phuoc Binh—which means "prosperity" and "peace." Tron showed Sarah letters from Larry Burrows. She stroked Sarah's hair as she held her hand.

Lau's and Kim Phúc's stories follow.

TRON'S SMILE IN THE YEAR 2000 (left) belies a hard life. She is working two jobs—as a tailor and a medic—in Phuoc Binh, where Larry Burrows's son, Russell, and Russell's daughter, Sarah, find her during a Vietnamese odyssey.

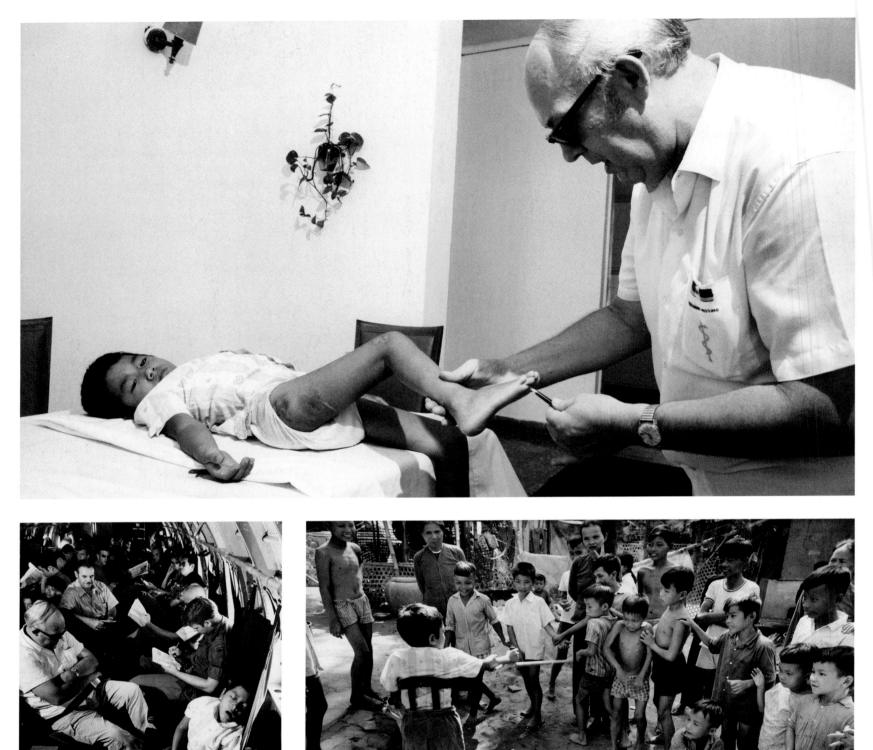

THE STORY OF THIS BOY was sad in 1970 when Larry Burrows learned of it and is no happier today—as far as we know. From LIFE's issue of January 29, 1971: "Nguyen Lau was seven years old and playing in a rice field one day in 1967 when a soldier—name and army unknown—quick-handed a bomb into a mortar tube. The explosion sent jagged metal fragments scything through the paddy. One by chance found Lau's puny backbone. Slicing through his spinal cord, it paralyzed him from the waist down and left him to face a slow death in a wretchedly equipped hospital. Eight months later, Lau was rescued." Sort of. An American group called the Committee of Responsibility, which was dedicated to helping child war victims, flew him to the United States for treatment. After three years, he was returned home. At top, Dr. Herman Wissing, a COR doctor who has accompanied Lau during the trans-global flight (above, left), checks Lau's nerve responses at the National Rehabilitation Institute in Saigon in September 1970. But in his village and even in reunion with his family, both Lau and Larry Burrows find that this boy, who has forgotten his native tongue, is scorned and taunted (above, right). Lau's subsequent fate is unknown.

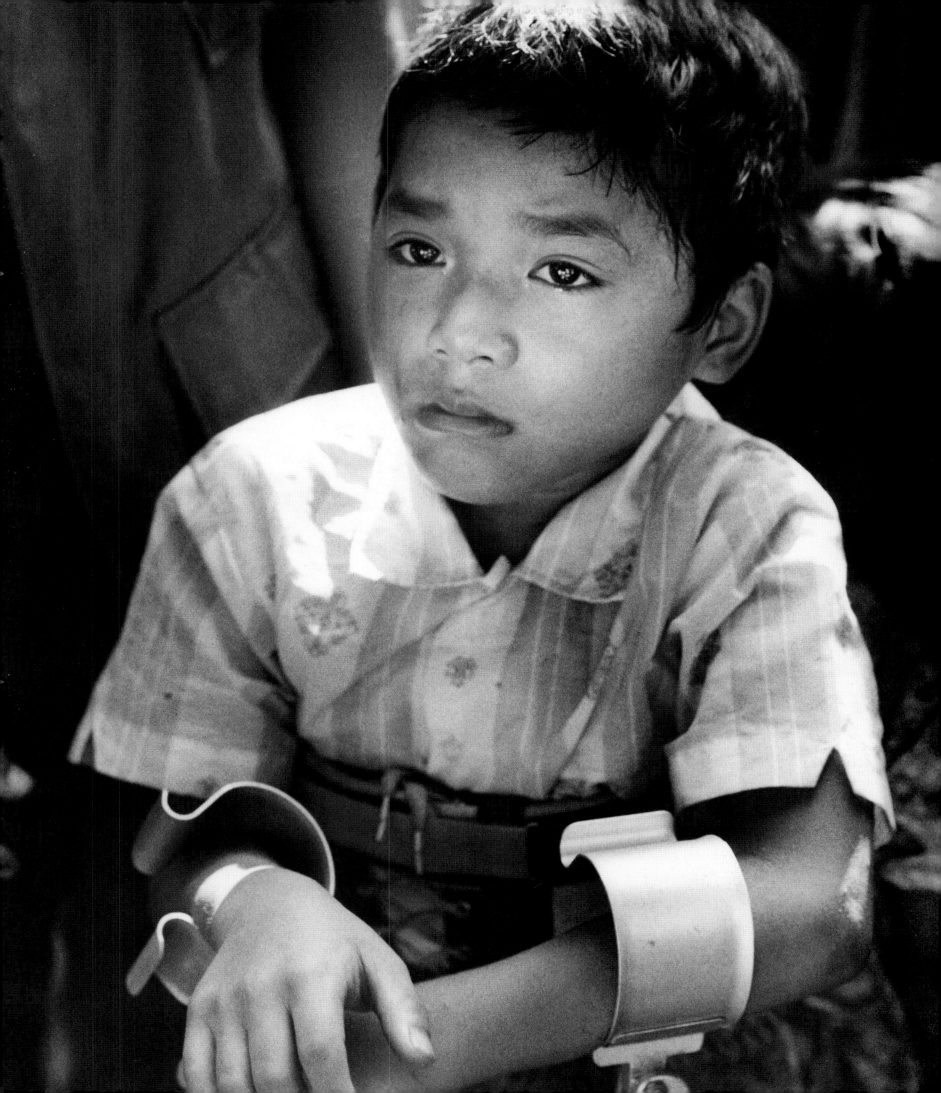

NICK UT/AP

JOE MCNALLY/LIFE

THIS IS CERTAINLY ONE OF THE MOST SEARING IMAGES
of the war, along with Burrows's "Reaching Out" (please see page 106),
Eddie Adams's "General Loan" (page 110), David Douglas Duncan's
"Con Thien" (page 102), and the work of Horst Faas, Henri Huet and
some few others. The photograph at left has become known simply as
"Napalm Girl," as we have noted, which serves to demean Phan Thi
Kim Phúc and the other children harmed here during an attack in 1972.
Some newspapers, it was said, hesitated to run Nick Ut's Associated
Press picture because Kim Phúc's clothes had been burned off,
but ultimately the image won the Pulitzer Prize. President Nixon said:
"I'm wondering if that was fixed." Ut replied: "The picture for me
and unquestionably for many others could not have been more real.
The photo was as authentic as the Vietnam War itself. The horror of the
Vietnam War recorded by me did not have to be fixed." As Ut pointed
out, "That terrified little girl is still alive today." Indeed, she now lives in
Canada, and she and Ut have visited many times through the years.
The photo above of Kim Phúc with her son Thomas was taken by
Joe McNally 23 years after Ut took the one at left. LIFE asked McNally
to find the subjects of a number of Pulitzer Prize–winning images,
and in 1995 he made this picture at the family's home in Toronto.

SURVIVORS

THE V SIGN, FLASHED WITH TWO FINGERS, almost always signified "victory" for U.S. forces heading home after any particular hard-fought war. On March 4, 1973, on a flight filled with released American prisoners of war departing Gia Lam airport in Hanoi and bound for Clark Air Base in the Philippines, it also meant "peace." That was what the protesters back home were signifying and seeking. Even in the military ranks, doubts about the reasons for fighting in Vietnam had increased, as had doubts about ultimate victory, as had, finally, outright dissension. Despite the complexities attending the war's end, there is a kind of jubilation in this picture. At the very least: great relief.

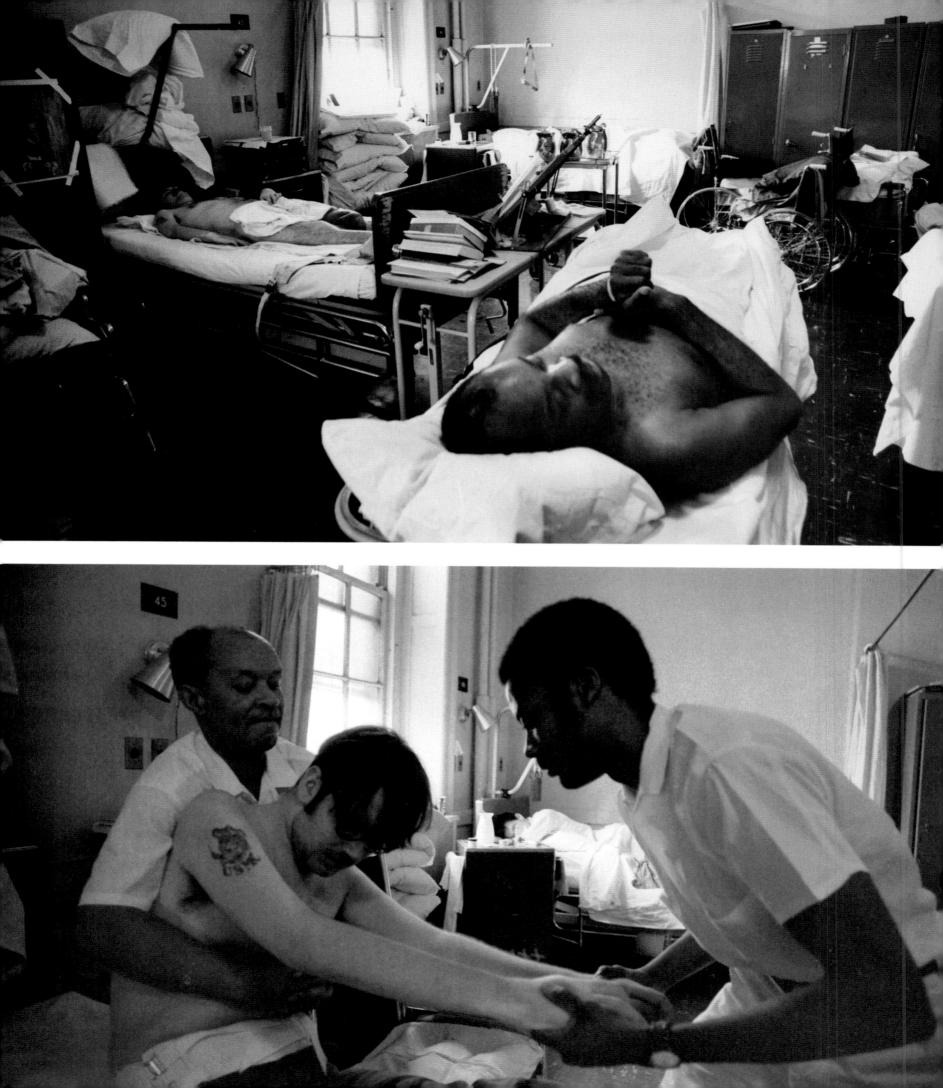

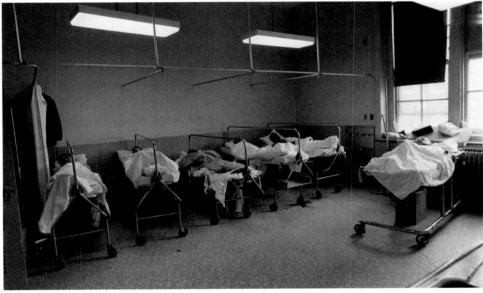

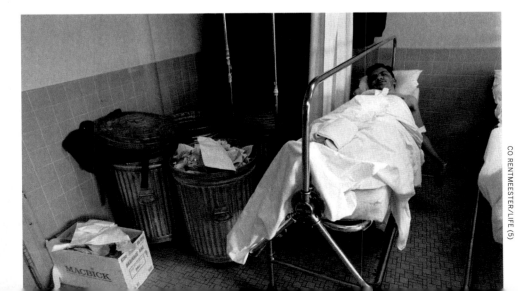

*urvivor.* That is a loaded word. It means a person who has persevered and made it through. It means a person who might have, at one point, faced long odds. It means a person who might have been nicked—in a significant way or a less significant way.

The former prisoners of war on the previous pages had surely been dealt a harsh blow, and the Medal of Honor recipients on the pages immediately following had each looked into the belly of the beast. The men in the five photographs on these two pages took a bullet for their country and now were home—or in their way station to home.

We as a nation might have learned that if we owe our war veterans nothing else, we owe them at least thanks, care and medical support—physical and psychological succor. But the recent scandals involving Veterans Administration hospitals and the treatment of troops returning from the Iraq and Afghanistan conflicts have a direct precursor in the later years of the Vietnam War. And so, it seems, we have learned little or nothing. A cover story by LIFE's Co Rentmeester in the May 22, 1970, issue provides, today, a very uncomfortable reminder.

Rentmeester had been in the field for much of the war; in this case he was back in the Bronx, New York, at the Veterans Administration hospital there. What he witnessed and documented stunned him—battle-hardened though he was. Consider: In the enema room of the hospital, seen at top left on this page, disabled spinal injury patients wait up to four hours to be attended to by a single aide. The year was 1970. The year now is 2014. These are survivors, yes—but do we help them survive? Do we encourage them to recover?

In 1970, LIFE asked if the war wounded were "fated to pass into the bleak backwaters of our Veterans Administration hospitals . . . A man hit in Vietnam has twice as good a chance of surviving as he did in Korea and World War II, as support hospitals perform miraculous repairs on injuries that tend to be more devastating than ever before. But having been saved by the best field medicine in history," one in seven wounded in Vietnam would enter the V.A. system, characterized then by LIFE as a "medical slum"—and today, by many, as the same.

After LIFE's article, there was a five-month inquiry by a Senate subcommittee. Gross inadequacies were found, and cutbacks to the V.A. budget were cited. A half century on, Congress is jawing again, and certainly similar blame will be assessed. Meanwhile, the survivors try to survive another day.

IN A PARTITIONLESS WARD (opposite, top), a disarray of dirty linen is allowed to pile up around a quadriplegic's bed while the patient lies naked, unable to clothe himself after a shower. In the bottom photograph and others on this page: More pictures that speak for themselves.

OUR BEST AND BRAVEST include, at top left, on January 16, 1969, Army Sergeant Drew Dennis Dix of Colorado, who is presented the Medal of Honor by President Lyndon Johnson as earlier honorees (from left) Navy Lieutenant Clyde E. Lassen of Florida, Marine Major Stephen Pless of Georgia and Air Force Lieutenant Colonel Joe Jackson, also of Georgia, stand at attention. Above, left: On December 19, 1966, Army Secretary Stanley R. Resor presents the Medal of Honor to First Lieutenant Walter J. Mar Jr. of Pennsylvania in a ceremony at the Pentagon; Mar is being cited for heroism in the battle in the Ia Drang Valley. Top right: Mrs. Lawrence Joel of North Carolina regards the Medal of Honor that President Johnson has presented to her husband, Army Specialist 6 Lawrence Joel. Cited for valor in helping the wounded while wounded himself, Joel is the first medical corpsman to receive the nation's highest decoration in the Vietnam War. Above, right: On March 18, 2014, President Barack Obama presents the Medal of Honor to Army Sergeant First Class José Rodela, one of 24 U.S. Army veterans awarded the medal for heroic action in combat during World War II, Korea and Vietnam. Nineteen of the 24 had already received a Distinguished Service Cross, but because of their racial or ethnic backgrounds had till now been overlooked for the Medal of Honor. Opposite, top: On May 16, 2012, former soldiers from the unit of Army Specialist Leslie Sabo Jr. watch as President Obama presents Rose Mary Sabo-Brown with the Medal of Honor posthumously to her husband for his brave deeds in Cambodia in May 1970. Sabo served as a rifleman with the 101st Airborne Division during the Vietnam War before he was killed in action. Bottom: In a photograph by Larry Burrows's son, Russell, made in 1999, retired Marine Gunnery Sergeant Jeremiah Purdie, who was the wounded soldier stumbling toward a wounded Marine in the famous 1966 photograph (please see page 106), touches the name of his former commanding officer at the Vietnam Veterans Memorial Wall. Purdie died in 2005 at age 74.

MEMORIAL

Like the war and the fallen warriors it commemorates, the monument in Washington was, from the first, different—and worked in different ways. Thirty-two years after it was dedicated, it is acclaimed as a fitting—in fact, perfect—tribute. LIFE's **Amy Lennard Goehner** talked recently with its creator, **Maya Lin.**

THE THINGS LEFT BEHIND at the Vietnam Veterans Memorial have been surprising and moving to Lin; she anticipated other aspects of the reaction to her wall, but not this. Opposite: A collection of dog tags that were included in a 1992 Smithsonian National Museum of American History exhibition that featured some 500 items from a collection of more than 25,000 objects left at the memorial. Even that substantial archive represents only a fraction of the 400,000 mementos deposited since the wall opened; each evening at sunset, National Park Service rangers carefully store the day's additions. The most common objects left are letters, notes and poems. Every type of medal awarded during the war, including one Congressional Medal of Honor, has been left. But one visitor left a large painted storm door, another a tiger's cage meant to represent the confinements POWs were kept in, another a bottle of Jack Daniel's whiskey. Several reel-to-reel tapes are filled with music of the time. Two sonograms of an unborn infant were found at the wall, with a note that read: "If the baby is a boy, he'll be named after you, Dad. This child will know you. Just how I have grown to know and love you, even though the last time I saw you, I was only four months old."

n 1981, Maya Lin was a 21-year-old architecture student at Yale University when her design for the Vietnam Veterans Memorial was chosen from among 1,421 entries in a competition. At its core, Lin's imagined monument was a simple, black granite *V*-shaped wall receding into the earth and etched with the names of the more than 58,000 U.S. men and women who gave their lives or remain missing. Visitors peering at the names could see their own tear-stained reflections in the stone.

If the memorial's simplicity belied its depth, this was not apparent at the time to all, and the design met with immediate controversy. From an issue of LIFE: "It is unlike any monument, especially the familiar white icons on the Mall to which it points . . . called a 'black gash' by one veteran, a 'nihilistic statement' by another . . . The fact that it had no heroic images, no flags, the fact that it was built into the earth instead of towering above it suggested to some that the wall was an insult, a cruel black line underscoring the nation's shame about the war that it didn't win."

Lin herself was attacked (she was a woman, she was too young, she was of Asian heritage), but she defended her vision of the memorial in public forums, even before Congress. The wall was built, and the passage of time has proved that Lin was right from the first. Four million visitors approach the wall every year; daily, people can be seen making rubbings of the names carved into the stone.

Lin has gone on to create other commanding installations, including the Civil Rights Memorial in Montgomery, Alabama, along with countless works in her dual careers in art and architecture. But she will always be known for the wall, and she is fine with this.

LIFE: You've surely received many letters through the years.
LIN: Some of the most compelling letters are the ones from psychiatrists who have worked with Vietnam vets. The war was so troubling, and they use a visit to the memorial as kind of their last step in recovery. I remember getting a couple of letters from psychiatrists saying thank you so much because what this allowed the veterans to do is to face something that at first they couldn't, but [as they] go through therapy, this is the culmination. This makes me feel really good, that a work like that could help people to that degree. I always think of my works on a very individual, personal level, and I didn't really think of this being a largely visited, popular site. But what I did know from the get-go: I knew with returning veterans, there was a very great chance that they were going to cry, they were going to be very moved. It was going to be very painful. But in a way what you have to go through is a facing of this loss, and experiencing the pain, in order to get better. That basically was the whole genesis of the wall: the psychological catharsis you have to go through. First, you have to face the reality of that war.

LIFE: How, given your age at the time . . . ?
LIN: I don't know. This is all about: How do we allow ourselves to mourn? We'd been studying this in a course at Yale—that the American culture tends to not look at dying or aging as part of the healing process, whereas in some older cultures, the ritual of mourning is very much a part of the life cycle. We are a young country and

a young culture, and we like looking to the future. We like looking to our youth. Not death.

Now add to that the trauma of what the returning veterans went through because [many] weren't accepted back into society. Protesters spat on them. They had to own their time in Vietnam almost as if it had been their responsibility. Rather than the country sheltering them and taking them back, they faced this. I think psychologically they had a really, really hard homecoming, and maybe I hoped to raise awareness, and have people face war and death, and acknowledge this group that came back.

I hadn't known anyone who died in the war, but I just knew. As I was working on it, the veterans would say, "What do you think people's first response is going to be?" I didn't tell them, but I was thinking, *There's a good chance a returning vet is going to cry.*

My own first experience of this—I'll never forget it—was on the day before the dedication, and I went down to the site and this huge Vietnam vet was very emotional, and he started yelling at me, basically pinning me at the apex, yelling, and actually they sent the rangers in [because] they were afraid for me. Part of me was afraid, the other part of me said, *It's working.* This fellow—maybe it is pulling out of him the emotions he needs to experience to overcome that war. This is about awareness of death. Eventually you have to turn around and walk into the light. It's through a mirror darkly: You are seeing the names of the dead, seeing into the darker world, but you must turn around and ascend back into the light.

LIFE: Do you visit the wall regularly?
LIN: When I go back I feel like I am a voyeur because it's not my place to be there. You are witnessing the thing you predicted would happen, and yet you don't want to be observing those families that have lost people. I choose to keep that distance.

I don't think [the reaction to the memorial] has surprised me. What's surprised me is people leaving things. I knew people

CHRIS MADDALONI/POLARIS

would touch the names, because part of the inspiration was that there was a rotunda at Yale called Woolsey Hall and you couldn't not touch the names. That is an emotional touchstone that I knew would happen. But the leaving of objects was something so beautiful. These works, once you build them, really do take on a life of their own. I love focusing on some of the important historical, social events—civil rights, women's rights, the environment—and presenting facts but leaving it up to you to come away with your own conclusions. I don't try to tell you what you are supposed to be coming away with. I think this creates a one-on-one experience with these pieces, and it asks each individual visitor to really participate to make the work whole.

And now they leave things.

LIFE: The memorial has affected many. Certainly, it changed your life.
LIN: Well, it's a big public work and I'm really glad that it's been as helpful as it's been, but it's a funny life I've led {laughs}. That's a pretty big piece coming out of the gate. I do think we tend as a culture to specialize and we like to label, and it's been a real juggling act to do everything I've wanted to do—art, architecture, the memorials—and not be typecast. I've been very fortunate, and I've done all three almost equally. For me they balance out. I see it as a tripod, and you couldn't take away one leg without the other two falling over.

We know there are left and right sides of the brain. I think the memorials are slap-dab in the middle. They require both sides. There is an incredible amount of research. For the Vietnam memorial, for instance, we had studied funeral architecture in school, so I understood the power within such works to communicate certain psychological or emotional responses. It was something that was and still is of great interest to me.

LIFE: Is there something you know now that might have helped you back then?
LIN: Actually, the exact opposite. I think if I had been who I am today back then, I might not have gotten through it. I think it took the beautiful naïveté of youth, where you know you are right and they are all wrong! {laughs} As a young person you have direct thoughts: *They don't need a parade, because a parade isn't going to make them feel better. They need honesty. They need to face this.*

Maybe as you get older, you have doubts. I think my youth really helped protect me.

At the time, when people would ask {about the memorial}, I'd say {to myself}, *I will focus on the design, but I'm not going to talk about the controversy because that's irrelevant.* What I didn't realize was that it

ADAM STOLTMAN/CORBIS

"ROLLING THUNDER" is no longer a bombing operation, as it had been during the war, but an annual motorcycle rally at the wall on Memorial Day weekend to remember prisoners of war and troops missing in action; in 2007 these pictures and mementoes (opposite) are some of the items left behind. Above: Lin in Barre, Vermont, at work on her Civil Rights Memorial for Montgomery, Alabama.

was all so hard and so traumatic that I was doing my own bottling. I cried on and off for a couple of weeks because, as I was experiencing it, I realized I was bottling it. I had been bottling the whole trauma of getting it built.

LIFE: That was your version of what the vets went through.
LIN: Yes, but not the same of course. What we did to the Vietnam vets . . . We sent them over there, they were kids, we trained them, then they came back, people spat on them, people blamed them for the war. So these poor kids ended up with a psychological rift.

What have we learned? Look at what the returning veteran today is going through. It just breaks my heart. I think: *Could we do better, please?* Because the returning vets from the last two wars have been cycled over and over, and the injury rate, and the suicide rate—I look at this and I go, *Have we learned anything? Can we not help these veterans who have given so much?*

I don't think we have learned that lesson. How can we be helping these returning veterans more? I think we are still turning our back to our veterans.

At least, a lot of people are talking about it.
I'm wondering: What can be done?

LIFE: Do they deserve a memorial?
LIN: I think they do, but it wouldn't be by me. Seriously, though: I think they need more than a memorial. They need a lot of support and help. What these vets are going through—coming home, some with all these new types of injuries. We've never seen anything like this. What needs to get done is: a lot more help.

REMEMBERING

LIFE magazine's last staff photographer in a long line was **Joe McNally,** who, like many of his predecessors, has a history of shooting in Indochina. He made the picture of the adult Phan Thi Kim Phúc with her infant son on page 147. LIFE Books asked him to visit veterans of all sides of the Vietnam War 50 years later. Accompanying Joe was LIFE's **Daniel S. Levy,** recording the thoughts of these men and women who had different answers to the essential question. Here, in 18 pages: McNally's photographs, Levy's reporting and the thoughts and tears of those who were engaged—a half century ago. The Vietnam War, today.

PAST BATTLES The Vietnam War ended more than four decades ago. But for many who fought in the jungles and mountains and on the plains of Southeast Asia—and on Main Street America—that era remains as deeply etched in their minds as the names on Washington, D.C.'s Vietnam Veterans Memorial.

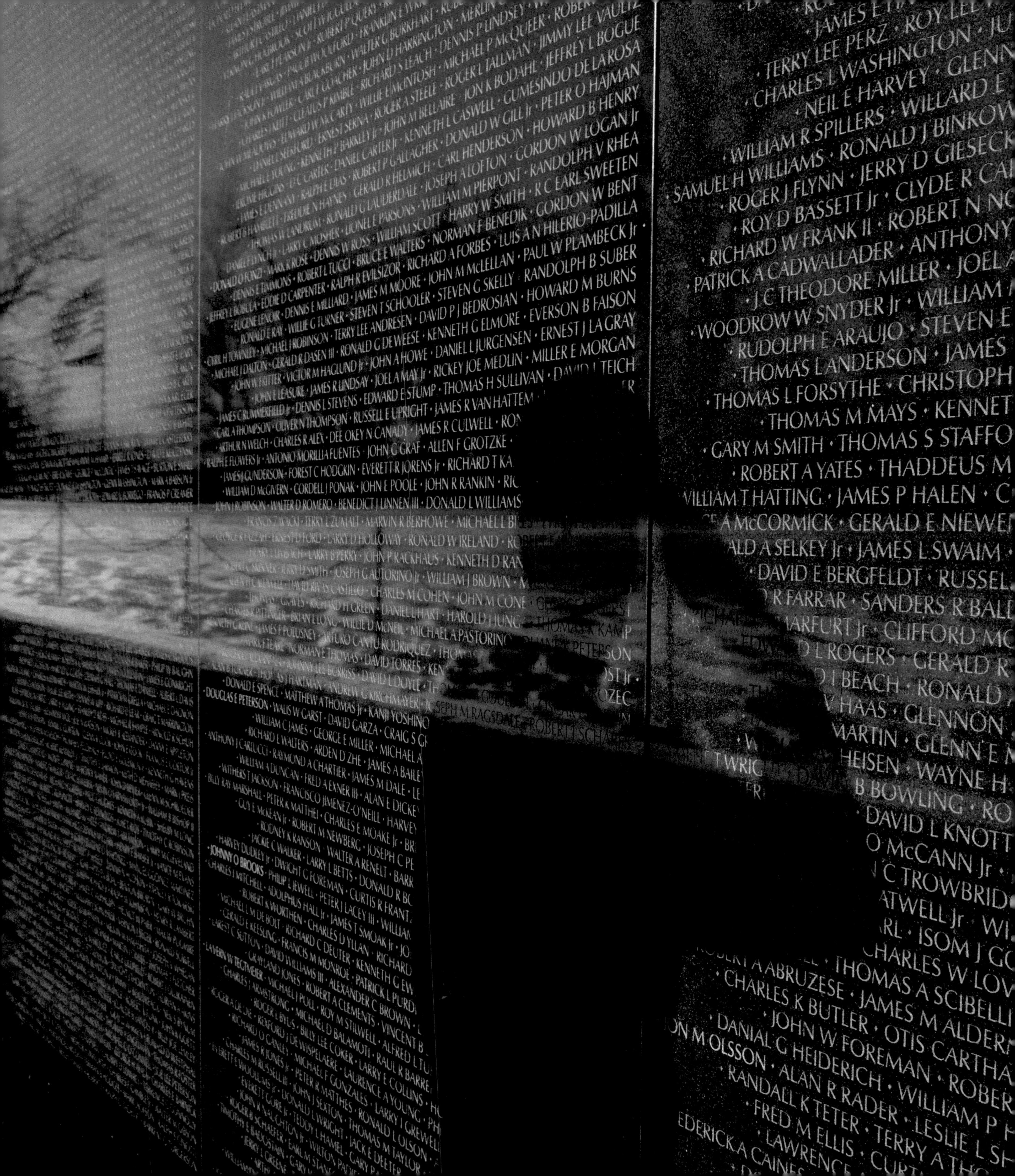

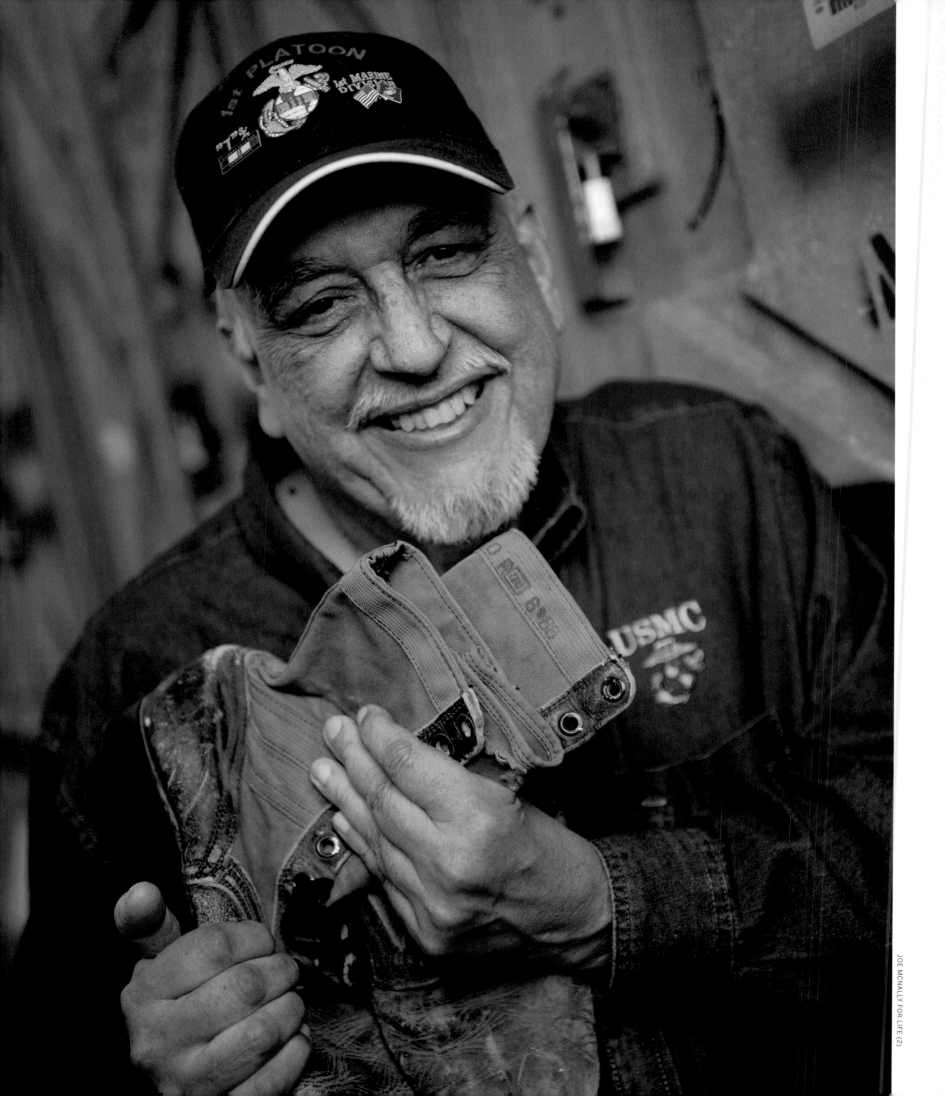

South Vietnam's Quang Nam Province was an especially deadly spot in November 1967 as Second Lieutenant Lawrence E. Wilson led the 35 Marines of India Company's 1st Platoon through its rural villages. "You didn't know exactly who the enemy was," recalls Gerard N. Dumont, the platoon's weapons squad leader. "They dressed like villagers, but they had AK-47s."

The men of India Company, 3/7, 1st Marine Division were 15 miles inland from the South China Sea taking part in Operation Foster: relocating villagers, searching for North Vietnamese and Vietcong, and destroying their supplies and equipment. "The overwhelming desire was to get these innocent civilians out of harm's way," says Bernard "Doc Mac" McNallen, the platoon's Navy Corpsman. Once they were moved, Wilson notes, "Our objective was to locate, capture or destroy the enemy." On the 19th the men—carrying machine guns, flak jackets, haversacks, rifles, bandoleers of ammo, canteens, and hand, smoke and tear gas grenades— were patrolling alongside a curling mile-and-a-half stretch of water they dubbed "Finger Lake" when a squad from India Company's 2nd Platoon was assaulted. Wilson's men rushed to help but came under fire and suffered 10 casualties. By nightfall, with the valiant help of the 3rd Platoon, they retrieved the injured.

At 5:00 a.m. on the 21st Wilson settled his men between the villages of Phu An and Phu Binh. The 2nd Platoon set up nearby, and the Marines planned to clear the enemy from the western edge of Finger Lake. Heavy undergrowth surrounded the hooches—straw and bamboo huts—and as light came up Wilson realized they were alone and out in the open. He spied movement, and Radioman Arthur Toy called the company commander, who said that the activity at the base of the lake was probably Marines. Yet Wilson, who at 23 had taken over as platoon commander in July, had his doubts. "They bounced as they walked," he observes. "Marines don't what we called 'Diddy Bop.' That was a telltale key that they were not friendly." His men confirmed his fears, but the commander advised against engaging them. "They are seeing enemy," remembers James Keene, a then-19-year-old rifleman from Del City, Oklahoma, "and we are starting to worry how in the world are we going to handle it."

The men moved to the tree line and swept the area, coming across abandoned hooches and fighting holes. At 11:30 they took a break. Corporal Dumont, who at 23 was on his second tour, guarded a trail entrance: "It was still and quiet," he recalls. It was so calm that Keene thought the enemy had decided to leave. Wilson rested with Toy and McNallen, a 21-year-old from Throgs Neck, New York, who today recalls: "We sat down to eat our 'C rats'"—the C rations that might be ham and lima beans or might be spaghetti. Corporal Leonard Calderon, a 27-year-old rifleman from Los Angeles,

sat down by a ditch to eat alongside Ira Hullihen. Keene was with Edward Welsh and remembers enjoying the ham and eggs: "They tasted pretty good cold or hot." When they finished, Wilson told the 2nd platoon that the 1st would lead. "I said, 'Okay. Let's saddle up.'"

As they did, "The whole tree line opened up with machine gun fire, small gun fire, mortar fire," says Wilson. The enemy shot AK-47 assault rifles and B-40 rockets, ripping the foliage and splintering the hooches. When Calderon heard the shooting he grabbed his M-16, rolled into the ditch and started shooting. Keene grabbed his M-14: "I hit the ground, crawled to cover and returned fire. They had us outnumbered." Dumont saw where the firing was coming from, and he tried "to figure out what we could do to counteract the situation."

The Marines, shielded by hooches, craters and grave mounds, fired back, tossed grenades and shot M79 grenade launchers. The enemy peppered the area with mortar shells. A bullet hit PFC Vaughn O'Neil in the chest. Shells and shrapnel pierced men's legs, backs and sides. Frantic shouts of "I'm hit" and "Corpsman" filled the air. McNallen rushed to help, but as he did he was briefly knocked unconscious. "When I came to, I made my way out around the hooch and saw O'Neil. He had a sucking chest wound. He was gasping and gurgling blood." McNallen used moistened cellophane from a cigarette pack to form a seal on the wound, but it would not hold and mouth-to-mouth did not work. The 21-year-old from Lincoln Park, Michigan, was choking, and McNallen shifted him to figure out what was wrong. "When I put him on his side his lungs fell out right in both of my hands." O'Neil still had a slight pulse, and McNallen wrapped him in a rubber poncho to hold his organs inside. "I knew him really well. I didn't want to see the guy die."

Wilson radioed the company commander, but the other platoons were likewise engaged. He had to establish "fire superiority" to set up a staging spot for the wounded, as well as establish a place to bring in a medevac helicopter. He and Toy moved to a rise by a

A WARRIOR REUNION of Leonard Calderon, James Keene, Lawrence Wilson, Gerard Dumont and Bernard McNallen at the Marine Corps Reserve Training Center in Pasadena, California, is seen above. The rifle was captured from a Vietcong. Opposite: Calderon with comrade R.M. "Cook" Barela's boots from Vietnam.

bomb crater. Keene and Welsh set up 15 yards away behind a small mound. Gunner R.M. "Cook" Barela and others returned fire. The shooting went on for 30 minutes or more. Wilson radioed an artillery battery 10 miles away, and soon artillery shells shook the earth.

"The wounded were all over the place," says McNallen. "Everyone is crying, screaming. Things are going off around you. You can hear incoming coming in. It is pretty spooky." A machine gun nestled 160 feet away fired on them from the tree line. It needed to be taken out, and Wilson called for the rocket team and contacted the Forward Air Controller, which dispatched a flight of Air Force McDonnell Douglas F-4 Phantoms. Wilson was warned that they were too close for regular bombs and was advised that they could drop napalm: "Some of your people might get hit." The lieutenant had no choice, telling the dispatcher, "We will take napalm." The jet swooped in just as the rocket team fired on the gunner. The napalm's surge of oxygen-sucking flames burst across the spot, as did a second drop, landing not far from Keene and others: "I felt the heat off of it. It put out such a huge ball of gassy flames, an intense heat of black smoke and flames."

Soon Marine A-4 Skyhawks dropped napalm and strafed the enemy with cucumber-sized projectiles. Wilson needed his men to charge the tree line and said to the pilot, "Give it to me again." But the planes had no more shells. The enemy didn't know that, and Wilson asked for a dry run. "We had to get in there while their heads were down." As the plane returned Wilson hollered to his men, "Go now!" The men "thought I must be crazy," but they followed their officer's orders. "One got up, and the next and the next" and charged the tree line. As Calderon ran he worried, *Do I have a full magazine? Do I have an empty magazine?* As he raced forward, he remembered how during practice assaults his instructor told the men to shout, "'Bang! Bang!' just like Cops and Robbers." Rushing through the brush Calderon saw Welsh alongside him. Welsh had run out of ammo, but Calderon heard him shouting, "Bang! Bang!"

Their assault scattered the enemy up the lake into a rice paddy. The airborne controller confirmed some 80 dead. By now Wilson had a dozen or so men left who were capable of fighting. He figured they had beaten their foes and soon heard the drone of an approaching CH-34 medevac helicopter. "They came down and were just about ready to land. All of a sudden I see metal flacking off the cowling," says Wilson. "It pulls back up and she goes off. I grabbed that horn. I started to yell at the pilot. Before I could get anything out, he says, 'The flight crew chief was just shot in the head. I am not coming back until you get everything cleared up.'"

It was late in the afternoon. McNallen tended to the wounded. His main worry was shock: "You can die over there quicker from shock than some wounds." O'Neil, though, was fading, his face turning ashen. McNallen comforted him. "They don't die with their eyes closed," the Corpsman solemnly recalls. "They die with their eyes open. There is a transition from eyes that are alive to eyes that are dead. That transition never goes away in your mind, even years later. You still see those eyes. You are the last one between him and dying."

Machine gunner Dennis Martinez told Wilson the shooting had come from a hooch in a rice paddy hidden by banana trees about a third of a mile away. He needed to help an Army Huey gunship locate the enemy. "I turned to my most trusted Marine," Wilson says, telling Dumont, "Jerry, grab some people, go out there and throw smoke on that hooch so we can mark it." One of the men he enlisted was PFC Charles Taylor III, a 19-year-old "gangly fellow" from Little Rock, Arkansas. Wilson told him: "When Dumont says, 'Go,' you go. Don't hesitate. Go!" The team zigzagged toward the enemy, and while crossing an open area a shot rang out. Dumont didn't hear the round and one of his men yelled, "Corporal Dumont. Stop! He got hit." Keene and Welsh pulled Taylor out of the rice paddy back to the safety of a mound behind some tall grass. With "a chopper waiting for the markings," Dumont knew, "it had to get done." He and the others continued. "As soon as we threw the smoke and saw it disperse, I said, 'Let's get the hell out of here.'"

When Wilson spotted the smoke he told the helicopter pilot, who said, "Yeah. I am going to knock the hell out of him," and he took out the hooch. Soon the men returned with Taylor. McNallen gave him mouth to mouth, but the young man had been struck in the head and could not be saved. Out of frustration, the Corpsman grabbed his Remington shotgun and fired randomly toward the enemy.

A medevac took away the wounded and dead. By then Wilson felt they had probably won the day, but as dusk descended, some of his men heard voices calling out, "Marine, you die tonight." Wilson feared another assault, perhaps even hand-to-hand combat, and told the remains of the 2nd Platoon to move in with the 1st Platoon and ordered everyone to "break out the gas masks and be ready." Calderon pulled out his mask and grabbed his Ka-Bar Marine fighting knife. "We were in trouble," he says. "You could actually see the enemy running back and forth between the trees." Keene set his bayonet on his rifle. Dumont distributed ammo. Wilson simply thought, *We have to stay alive,* and told the company commander, "I don't think we are going to make it through the night."

McNallen recalls: "I honestly looked up to the sky and said, 'God, you are going to lose me.'"

It was about 7:00 p.m. when they heard the distant drone of helicopters. The Corpsman asked, "Are they coming here? Do you think?" Yes: The flight of CH-46 helicopters with about 150 Marines was coming for them. When First Lieutenant Charles Chritton saw the sprawling enemy bodies and the condition of Wilson's platoon, he told him, "You guys have done enough and can rest tonight." Wilson says today, "We stayed there. He took care of us."

Only 12 of the 1st Platoon's 35 members got out of Finger Lake without serious injuries. Two were killed. It was later learned that the enemy lost about 300 men. Wilson's men nominated him for a Bronze Star with a "V" for valor, an award he views as "one of the most important accolades of my life. Not because of its status as a medal but that it came from my men in recognition for what I did that day to keep them alive. I treasure that." The men freely acknowledge Wilson's efforts in that far-off land. "He cared about his people," says Keene. "There is no doubt his actions gave us a fighting chance to get out of there alive."

Says Dumont: "He was one heck of an outstanding platoon leader."

TALISMANS include, clockwise from top left, McNallen's Navy Commendation Medal with a Combat V, Dumont's boot camp photo, Wilson's map of Finger Lake and Keene's Marine Corps tattoos.

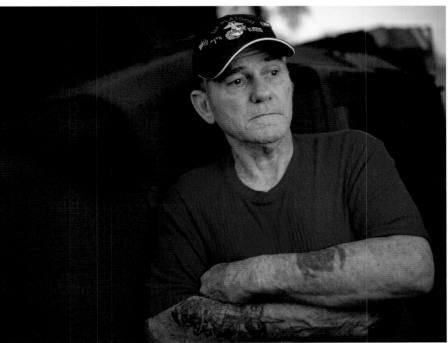

As has been made clear in these pages, LIFE is, this half century later, revisiting both of the Vietnam wars, the one that was ongoing over there and the other here at home. To that end, McNally and Levy recently visited not only former military men but combatants who were involved in the domestic discord. Richard Flacks was, in the 1960s, teaching at the University of Chicago and the University of California, Santa Barbara, and was a cofounder of the famous Students for a Democratic Society. Vivian Rothstein was a community activist. Abe Peck was a member of Chicago's underground press. Ross Canton was a decorated soldier who, upon returning home, joined the Vietnam Veterans Against the War. Here, during a sit-down with Levy in Santa Barbara, California, this group discusses not only their shared antiwar past but how they view their legacy today.

LIFE: How did you get involved in the antiwar movement?
ROTHSTEIN: I got recruited in the Mississippi freedom summer program in 1965. I decided I wanted to be an organizer. Then I got invited by Tom Hayden to go to a conference in 1967 in Bratislava, Czechoslovakia, to meet representatives of the provisional revolutionary government in South Vietnam, to actually meet the grass-roots opposition in South Vietnam. From that I got invited to go to North Vietnam. The experience crystalized my commitment to end the war.
CANTON: I was one of those poor white draftees. I was neutral with the war, until I got drafted. My first day out in the field in Vietnam our point man got wounded by a nine-year-old kid, and I thought, *So that's the enemy?* I was in the field three weeks when I got wounded the first time. The third time I spent nine and a half months in the hospital. I had shrapnel in my brain and was not supposed to survive. But I did. It crystallized my feelings about the war and how I was very angry. Once I got out I joined the Monterey chapter of the Vietnam Veterans Against the War.
FLACKS: I went to teach at the University of Chicago in 1964. A few months later a group of people in Ann Arbor [Michigan] started the action, which they called a "teach-in." Classrooms were used for

DAYS OF PROTEST are recalled at a roundtable by Vivian Rothstein, Richard Flacks, Abe Peck and Ross Canton in Santa Barbara, California. Copies of *The Chicago Seed,* the underground newspaper that Peck edited, are among mementos of the era.

debate, discussion, forums about the war. By the end of the academic year there were a thousand campuses where something like a teach-in had occurred. To me, that was the step I needed. I then devoted a great deal of my energy to being active in that role as a professor and as a campus leader.

PECK: I tumbled into the movement. I went to the Summer of Love in San Francisco, five guys in a Volkswagen van. My pivotal moment was driving to the Pentagon Demonstration in 1967. I saw everything from people putting flowers in guns to people storming the building to just having a sense of just how outraged we all were by the war.

LIFE: What did your families think of this?

FLACKS: My parents were schoolteachers in New York, active in building a union. In the McCarthy Red Scare era, they both were purged along with several hundred other left-wing, commie-oriented teachers. I was 25 by the time I was taking a stand against the war. They supported me.

CANTON: I grew up with a single mother who did the best she could. My father, an Italian immigrant, joined WWII early on, and was in the 101st Airborne for five years. Got wounded. He would have been prowar.

PECK: My parents weren't radicals at all. My dad was a liberal Democrat, very working class.

ROTHSTEIN: My mother had a progressive heart, but we were raised with this sense that we lived in an ominous world that could turn against you at any moment. But when she heard me speak about my trip to Vietnam, she got herself involved.

LIFE: Describe the time, if you would.

ROTHSTEIN: When I went away to college that first fall, Kennedy got shot. There was a sense that it was a chaotic political environment. We weren't being told what was going on. That engagement in the civil rights movement and the free speech movement gave the feeling that you could actually make a difference, that you needed to take a stand. I think we felt a sense that we could actually help end the war.

FLACKS: The draft was an expression of this militaristic, imperial power that we were opposed to. I was in the early founding of the Students for a Democratic Society. We thought we were responsible for having to have an antiwar movement. We thought the demonstrations of larger numbers of people would have an effect on policy, and that was perhaps naïve. A new lever that SDS perceived for a change of the policy was people being forced to fight the war had the opportunity to resist it. It was a strategic kind of effort: We who were in opposition to the war, if we ourselves refused to fight, and got other people to refuse to fight, the policy would have to be reexamined.

PECK: A lot of it was exhilarating, the idea that you could set the country on the right way, change the world, build a new society, stop the war. There was a concept of "right action"—that this was really the thing to do. I had great trepidation about the Chicago Convention in 1968, but I still had to go to the park. You had to show up.

LIFE: Did dissidents have regular contact with the veterans?
ROTHSTEIN: There was the GI coffeehouse movement. These were independent coffeehouses that were set outside the bases. Women staffed those. I helped to recruit people. I worked at Fort Leonard Wood. The idea was not to push any kind of line. But there was antiwar material there and underground newspapers. It was a very subversive strategy, because it was a place where guys could talk about what was really going on. It was brilliant.

PECK: There was this kind of ring around the military to support people making decisions of conscience.

CANTON: Returning veterans who were against the war were very dangerous, because we could tell what was true and what was not true. The whole idea of winning the war was deflated by all these Vietnam veterans coming back and saying that is not true. That really took hold. After [I spent] time in the hospital, I went back to Fort Ord and trained troops to go to Vietnam. We gave them the straight line. We told them that it was all bullshit.

LIFE: What was your experience with the mistreatment of vets?
CANTON: It never happened to any of the Vietnam veterans I was associated with—getting spit on at the airport, "baby killer!" and all those kinds of things. By 1969 there was a coalescence of trying to have the veterans and the soldiers be a part of the antiwar movement and not disenfranchising them because they served over there.

LIFE: How were women in the antiwar movement viewed?
ROTHSTEIN: The [anti] draft movement was very focused on men. Eventually we started building independent women's organizations and did antiwar activities. Women Strike for Peace was in there from the very beginning, the Women's International League for Peace and Freedom and the Jeannette Rankin Brigade.

LIFE: If so many opposed the war, why was it so hard to stop?
FLACKS: Both Johnson and Nixon said explicitly that no matter what public opinion said about the war, it would go on. It really [defies] explanation why, in the face of a popular mood against the war, these Presidents would feel they had to continue it. Vivian and I went to this conference in Bratislava, meeting the Vietcong, the North Vietnamese folks. They wanted to tell us that the U.S. had been defeated in the war, that there was no conceivable military strategy that the U.S. could deploy that would allow the U.S. to win. There was insight there into the limits of American power. It was reinforced a few months later during the Tet Offensive.

LIFE: So, at the end of the day, were all the protests useful?
FLACKS: If you add up the numbers of protests after Kent State, it is the largest mass demonstration in American history.
ROTHSTEIN: The amazing thing is hundreds of thousands of Americans took to the streets to oppose this war. That they cared that much, that they would put themselves at risk—it is really remarkable. What could you think of today where hundreds of thousands of Americans would get up off their couches and demonstrate?
PECK: A lot of good things came out of that period amid the tumult and the personal destruction.
ROTHSTEIN: Things have changed. There is no draft. Nobody can get over there to meet with the enemy and see what is going on. The press has to be embedded. They have changed the conditions.

LIFE: Talk about the radicalization and splintering of the movement.
ROTHSTEIN: There was all this chaos. The black communities were exploding. Martin Luther King was assassinated. Bobby Kennedy was assassinated. There was a lot of agitation. There was a lot of militancy on campus, and the repression came in—Kent State, the murder of Freddie Hampton in Chicago, the attacks on demonstrators at the Democratic Convention. People felt like they were coming to get us. People felt like the stakes were really high, and we weren't winning on the civil rights front, we were not winning on the antiwar front. I think some people became adventurist because they couldn't figure out a strategy that was going to work. It was a totally wrong strategy. You don't end an international conflict by breaking storefront windows.
PECK: People got extraordinarily frustrated. There were internal revolutions. It splintered . . . It was almost a Revolution of the Week Club.
CANTON: We were having infiltrators. The FBI parked out in front of my house. Everybody who was a leader in the Monterey chapter of the Vietnam Veterans Against the War had their phones tapped and were followed.
PECK: During the Democratic Convention our paper's windows were shot out and the only car on the street was a police car. The FBI came to look for my parents to find out more about me. They couldn't find my parents, but they found Mrs. Schwartz, my

neighbor. And they asked, "What kind of boy was he?" and she said, "Oh, he always held the elevator doors."

FLACKS: The founding people and elected leaders of the Students for a Democratic Society were on [an FBI] list. In May 1969, a guy called me who said he was a newspaper reporter wanting to interview me about student protests. He attacked me . . . and left me there bleeding. There was the Legion of Justice, a vigilante group. There is circumstantial evidence they were perpetrating this kind of activity and operating in connection with government intelligence.

ROTHSTEIN: I was organizing youth in Berwyn and Cicero, Illinois. We started a coffeehouse in a church, and the Legion of Justice shot crossbow arrows into the church. They found it so threatening that young people would sit and just talk about life, the draft or maybe whether they wanted to go to college. Nobody got hit. I remember going into meetings and being greeted by the Chicago police officer who was with the Chicago Red Squad, "Hey, Vivian. How are you doing?" They knew every person's name.

FLACKS: Whatever splintering there was, there was [also] a thread of more strategic action. People like Tom Hayden, Jane Fonda and others organized a campaign to get Congress to stop appropriating money for the war. And that was successful.

The shocking thing is that the American majority turned against the war in the late '60s. The morale of the troops was collapsing by the late '60s. Establishment intellectuals were writing about how the youth of America was turning against the society. And yet it *still* took six years for the war to be brought to an end after that.

LIFE: Looking back, your final thoughts?

PECK: I don't have laments. We were learning as we went. As the Grateful Dead would say, it certainly was a long, strange trip. Being in the underground press gave me a really enduring appreciation of the First Amendment, which I have always defended since then.

ROTHSTEIN: For years I was very fearful that anybody would know about me going to North Vietnam. In those days it was considered a traitorous thing to do. Now it's a really great thing to say I did. When I was in Vietnam, the Vietnamese said, "You are the true sons and daughters of Washington and Jefferson." They had a real sense of an American tradition. I think in retrospect, what I did was in the best interests of the country.

Looking back now, we can all be proud we took those risks, but at that time we had no idea what it would be like in 40 or 50 years. I feel proud of the things that I did. I feel it took too long to end the war. I think history has not really taken on the Vietnam War and

JOE McNALLY FOR LIFE

FBI FILES were compiled on all sorts of people in the 1960s, and here Peck, whose time in the underground press gave him an appreciation of the First Amendment, has his.

how right we were about the enormous destruction of Vietnam and the destruction it caused in our country. The antiwar movement is really not given the credit that I think we deserve.

PECK: There is no antiwar memorial.

FLACKS: I would argue that at the time, the best interests of this country were not served by a leadership getting us into war but [by] the people who were trying to stop the war. [Also] I have a positive view of some of the changes in society that have come out of this period. The idea that the U.S. should fight that kind of war is illegitimate now. The draft is illegitimate. I can't imagine a possibility of reviving conscription in this society. I know in my bones that if the move to restore the draft was made, there would be massive protests on college campuses right away.

The Vietnam War ended the capacity of people to be innocent and hopeful about political leaders. There is something healthy about that skepticism.

CANTON: The reason we were out protesting was because we cared. It was about caring for certain types of freedoms—caring about certain things that were being done in our name. Most of us, our parents were immigrants who really came here for the American Dream. We grew up with that idea that it would be a new country, a new world and a better world. And it *was* a better world.

PECK: On a good day we wanted America to live up to its promise.

CANTON: Yes. Exactly.

For this third part of our chapter on remembrance, photographer McNally and writer-reporter Levy gathered a number of people at the Wall, the Vietnam Veterans Memorial in Washington, D.C. They had prearranged a talk with Julian Bond. The lifelong social activist and Georgia state representative and senator had been, at Morehouse College in the late 1950s and early 1960s, one of the founders of the Student Nonviolent Coordinating Committee. He went on to be a 12-year chairman of the National Association for the Advancement of Colored People and was the first president of the Southern Poverty Law Center.

The testimony of Bond and others at the Wall follows.

JULIAN BOND: "I generally visit when friends are in town and I am showing them around. I thought it was genius to do what Maya Lin did. The Vietnam War was a divisive and unpopular thing. If you believe, as I do, that the whole thing was a terrible mistake, this is a reminder of that mistake and the cost we paid for this terrible, terrible mistake and a reminder that we ought to not ever do this again. It is probably a lesson not well learned.

"You walk down into it and you are getting into it, and you say, 'Look at the names grow, the people who died there get bigger and bigger and bigger.' And then they diminish as you walk out the other side. It is a great way to say we are putting this behind us. We are not forgetting the people or what they did, but we are putting the event behind us.

"I don't know anybody who died in Vietnam. Every time I go to the Wall I think of that because almost everybody I know knows somebody who died in Vietnam. I think it odd that I am not one of them. [But] when I go there, there is always someone taking a rubbing of somebody's name, and you think for these people: *This is a wonderful way to say, 'I knew John or Phil or Bob, and I want to commemorate the service he gave us. I can do it in this way.'*"

CHARLES SHYAB was a senior medic in the Army Infantry; a junior in college in 1966, he dropped out and was drafted, and the Army trained him to be a medic: "I went in as a conscientious objector. I didn't carry a weapon, but I still did my job. I feel proud." He served in the military from June 1967 until April 1969 and in Vietnam for six months of his service. He recalls: "I was in the Valley of the Shadow of Death and I came through. Some of my buddies didn't." Shyab was wounded at Chu Moor Mountain in April 1968, hit with shrapnel in the arms and legs. He doesn't remember much of being wounded, but "I remember getting on the copter. I went to a field hospital, and I remember the nurse who took care of me." In 2012, Shyab was awarded a Bronze Star for Valor for saving the lives of other soldiers during that battle. His friend Richard Cassano, who brought Shyab to the helicopter, never made it back to his foxhole, and Shyab regularly thinks of comrades like Cassano who were lost: "They were beautiful people . . . They will be 19 and 20 years old forever. There is not a day that goes by that you can't help but think

AT THE WALL are activist Julian Bond, top, and, below, veterans at a ceremony in February 2014.

about it." He feels that he came back because God was watching over him. "I felt that heaven was on my side. I am thankful to the Lord for still being alive. It was the Lord's care that [enabled me] to endure that." He does not warmly remember his return home: "When I was in school, people never asked me about it or wanted to hear me say anything. We blended in. It was sort of something to be ashamed of, not to be brought up or discussed." A half century later, he says, things have changed: "I have a Vietnam hat, and when people see my hat they thank me for my service. Afghanistan and Iraq vets give me acknowledgment."

ABRAHAM FULLER was a buck sergeant in the Army, serving in the military from 1964 until 1970 and in Vietnam from 1967 to 1969; he served in the Central Highland area, looking after infantry divisions and airborne units: "It was very ugly, dirty and very dangerous at times. It wasn't a nice job . . . If there was a firefight and there was believed to be American troops involved, we would be on our way to retrieve the estimated number of bodies that were in that area. We would get a sheet saying 'approximately 30 bodies,' and then we would have that many body bags. We came by helicopter or however we could get there. It was unpredictable if it was 'hot' or 'safe.' Most of the time they said it was safe, but it was never safe. Something that was supposed to be 'cold' could get 'hot' real quick.

"That war was hell over there. I was 22 going on 23. You did things we couldn't think about doing today. I blacked a lot of this stuff out of my mind. I am getting the worst end of things now: I don't sleep. I am not the same person I used to be. I used to be an entertainer and more outgoing. I have become more withdrawn. I was different when I came home. [But] I liked the Army. We used to play 'Army' when we were kids until it got dark. Army was in my blood. I have a brother who was in Vietnam. We were in Vietnam about the same time. I am glad I served my country."

FREDERICK J. EZELL was an Army sergeant who served in Vietnam for one year beginning in July 1969: "I was pretty young. We didn't always understand why we were there, but we knew what to do. I was on the Cambodian border on the western side of Vietnam. We went into Cambodia in May and June of 1970. It was really strange. It seemed like not only a different country but a different planet. It took me four weeks to get used to 98 degrees every day. Then there were the monsoons. It would rain every day at three o'clock. A huge sheet of water would come down. When it stopped you would be dry in 10 minutes. It was a strange place.

"You had a week of nothing happening and then a week of everything happening. I remember bad things mostly. I had a friend, he got hit by mortars, and he got ripped apart. The medics took him away. I never saw him again. That does not go away. Every now and then [an incoming round] would hit close and knock me down on the ground. My memories really were of trying to stay safe and trying to stay alive. You become fatalistic. I didn't think I was going to come back to the World. We called it the World—'coming back to the World.'"

ROBERT L. HOHMAN was an Air Force B-52 bomber commander who served in the military for 23 years beginning in 1962:

"I was from a blue-collar family. I felt I was very privileged to go to pilot training. It was a big step up for me. It was a privilege to serve in the military. I loved the military. The B-52 was the King of Battle, and at the time I was a very enthusiastic warrior.

"After the war and being around government I started to think, Why did we lose? For the last 30 years I have been trying to understand what we lost. I am conscious of the faults of our leadership at the time. We did some things right and we did some things wrong. We killed too many civilians. We [didn't] understand these insurgency issues well enough. The problem with Vietnam is we were dealing with an insurgency operation, and we were careful not to set off certain trip wires that would force us into a nuclear war with Russia and China. There were constraints to fighting a war without it escalating into a nuclear war."

TOM BURCH was a Green Beret lawyer; when the Tet Offensive began in early 1968 he was the judge advocate for Special Forces in the headquarters in Nah Trang: "It was not the combat experience that affected my whole life. It was the coming home experience. You felt that your family and friends would welcome you. Thirty-five percent of my Vietnam friends were spit on within 48 hours of coming home. When I came home no member of my family met with me. I got spit on. I couldn't get a job. I sent out résumés, and I put on there that I was in the military, and I didn't get any interviews. When I didn't put it on the résumé I got five interviews. I had post-traumatic stress disorder over that. You thought you would come home and it was a prestigious thing. Then I come home and go to a first-class restaurant wearing my uniform and four people started spitting on me. The girl I was with would never see me again. In 1971 I got stationed in the Pentagon. I had to do a lot of traveling, and I got written orders to no longer wear my uniform when I traveled since there were so many incidents. I was totally dismayed. I never dreamed that the public would treat us like that." Burch is convinced that there are still American POWs in Southeast Asia. "There were men left. There are still men being held in Laos, and the government is not doing anything about it. The Defense Intelligence Agency does whatever they can to keep that information from coming out."

LEN L. FUNK was an Army captain who served in the military from March 1967 until February 1971 and was an adviser in the northern section of the Mekong Delta: "I felt in the early part of the war that we were doing well. I was honored to be an adviser. I was fortunate to have learned the Vietnamese language and to be with the Vietnamese. We helped them. We passed on intelligence. We were with them on operations. We coordinated air strikes for them. We called in air support, either using the Vietnamese Air Force or the U.S. Navy." He came to feel differently about what evolved into "a God-awful guerrilla war with no defined line. When the Vietnamese were overrun it was their children who were killed. A frustrating thing was that when you came back it was so amazing how little the American people knew about the war. Americans didn't realize that the South Vietnamese lost a few hundred thousand people. Think of all the Vietnamese who died."

CHARLES HARRIS, who reached the rank of lieutenant colonel in his Army career, recalls: "I got my draft notice just before Thanksgiving in 1965. I did a lot of flying. I love to fly. I was at Hamburger Hill. I was getting toward the end of my year. It was a little tense. We all tracked our days to get out. Our commander wanted to be the next General Patton, and he kept having us doing foolish things. In 1971 to 1972, I was with the First Cavalry. I was an Air Mission Commander of an assault helicopter at An Loc when they were attacking Saigon. I was a platoon leader. We went to Da Nang and helped the South Vietnamese retake Quang Tri.

"The military was great for me. I got my undergraduate and graduate degrees. I got to see and do a lot of stuff. I am proud of it.

"Every five years we read the names on the Wall. I am not into that stuff, but my flight school roommate was killed in 1968, and in 1972 a good friend was killed. I read their names."

"I had hoped that we had learned something from the Vietnam thing. For their deaths to have been worth it, I thought as a nation we learned when to commit forces and when not to. Iraq blew that away. Each generation has to learn these things for themselves. That is very disheartening. In the modern wars we have held the soldier in high esteem. We did learn that from Vietnam and that has stuck. The lesson I wish we learned was a prudent use of American military—to really know what we were fighting for and what they are fighting for. We didn't seem to learn, and that is very disappointing.

"I believe I owe a huge debt of gratitude to those who raised their voices to get us out of Vietnam. They don't get the recognition they deserve—the people who stood up for those things. There are no statues or medals [for them]. I feel I owe those people a huge debt of gratitude."

WILBUR FLETCHER JR. was a private first class in the Army during his Vietnam service: "I was Graves Registration. We picked up the remains. It was a job. It wasn't something that I wanted to do. But they trained me for that and then they shipped me out. It was grim work. We handled the bodies. They came to us in the green bags. We had to do paperwork on that person. If they had watches, rings, we then had to process that and put it in an envelope. If we have a dog tag, we know who they are. If we didn't he was a John Doe. They were real unknowns, just like the Unknown Soldier. We processed whoever, we didn't care if was an enemy or the friend. The remains, the personal effects, we processed those. The processing for the American soldiers was down in Saigon. Our enemies went to another air base. We did Thai, Cambodian, Vietnamese, Vietcong, we did the whole deal.

"When I got in country, I had heart and I had feelings. But when it went along, I didn't have any feelings. If you go out into a war zone you are not going to be the same person as when you come back. I am still dealing with the PTSD. I have sessions every week where I go in and we have a roundtable. We talk about life. We try to stay away from Vietnam. Vietnam can dredge up some mean things in your mind. I found that it is something that you will never, ever lose.

SHARING MEMORIES at the memorial are, from top, veterans Tom Burch, Hubert Jordan and Charles Harris.

"That was a war to me that we shouldn't have even been in. We shouldn't have been there. It was a waste of time, money and lives."

ALBERT JENKINS was an Army Infantry specialist in Vietnam in 1967 and '68: "I was in supplies. We had to take supplies to the troops in the field. You would go out, stay two nights and come back. Wherever they moved, you had to bring supplies to them. There were maybe 20 trucks. We had minesweepers go ahead of us. The camp we were at was always hit at night. I was scared as hell when I went on convoy; you always thought about coming back alive. I recall the truck behind us got mortared. It was maybe five to 10 yards behind us. You heard a big bang, and you knew it was behind you and you turned around. It was so frightening.

"When we were leaving Vietnam there were two planes on the field. We took the first plane. When we got to Okinawa they told us that the other plane on the runway got hit. I think I could have been on the second plane, and I think about the people on the second plane. At nights you think about those who got hurt. Even if you didn't know them you felt like they were family.

"The veterans, when we got back, were called baby killers, and people acted as if we did something bad. But we did what we were called to do and asked to do. I was proud to do what I was called on to do as an American. I want people to know that we fought like hell for this country and we were welcomed home poorly."

MELVIN HAYES was an Army specialist with Field Artillery in the Mekong Delta in 1969: "We shot mortars where our troops needed them. We gave them support. Sometimes we had to shoot mortars on top of our troops because they were in a deep firefight. I was in a couple of firefights. We could see the bullets coming at us.

"[Post-traumatic stress disorder] has dampened my life. I could have accomplished more than I did. The V.A. Hospital has helped me to cope with the flashbacks. A lot of the kids: We train them to kill, and we then put them back in civilian life. They should be retrained to come back to civilian life.

"It took a long time, but people now say, 'Thank you for being in the war.' But the younger people don't know what went on during the Vietnam War. I would like them to know so they could understand what we went through and how we are trying to adjust."

TOM STRYER spent 20 years in the Navy beginning in 1965, rising to the rank of lieutenant commander, and served in Vietnam for a year beginning in April 1967: "I just turned 23 before I got into the country. I was the third oldest guy in my organization. These were young kids. They did their duty in good spirits. My best gunner was a cook. He was from Tennessee and grew up with a rifle across his knees. Put him on a 50 and he could write his name at about a mile away.

A GATHERING of those paying their respects on this particular day in early 2014 includes, opposite, top, Charles Shyab, and, bottom, second from left, Albert Jenkins. Next to him is Wilbur Fletcher. Abraham Fuller is kneeling. Luther Johnson, Melvin Hayes, Harold Hammond, Frederick Ezell and others are also shown. Right, from top: Jenkins, Robert Hohman and Tom Stryer.

JOE McNALLY FOR LIFE

"We were using the same kind of boats that they were using during D-Day in World War II. We did special ops. We did assaults a few times a week. We patrolled constantly. One of my duties was the water-side security for the base. We patrolled 12 miles up and down the river there. I had a piece of river that belonged to me. It was on the My Tho branch of the Mekong River. At the base we got mortared about four nights a week. At first it was very scary, then you got used to it. The typical attack was four to five rounds. It was done more to piss us off.

"I went out with a Navy corpsman and an Army doctor and gave medical treatment to villages four times a week. The idea was 'to know Americans, you have to love us.' We treated everyone who came in, from bullet and shrapnel wounds to dysentery to typhoid.

"Tet: We were firing rounds as fast as they could be loaded. We were relatively secure: There were a lot of mines that they had to get through, and they weren't very successful. None of the bad guys got as far as the fence. They opened up at about quarter to 11 and kept on coming in till five in the morning. By that time it was a mortar round every minute or two. Five thousand of them tried to get access to our base. The base was very defensible. We didn't find a single body, but we found a hell of a lot of body parts.

"A couple of days later we got to some of the villages that we typically visited, and there were folks there who were friendly to us. The villages were completely deserted. I think they were killed. These folks wanted nothing more than to be left alone by everybody."

HUBERT JORDAN was a private first class during his time in Vietnam in 1968 and 1969: "I come from a family of citizen soldiers. My ancestors fought in every war that America has fought in except for the Spanish-American War.

"My job in Vietnam was to calculate the data used by the artillery to fire on targets. The Fire Direction Center was the center of battery operations. We were the nerve center of the battery. This was a very intense job. I became a section chief responsible for supervising the operation of the FDC. If we made a mistake we could end up killing our own troops. There were those moments of sheer terror punctuated by relative calm. My position was overrun three times by the NVA [North Vietnamese Army]. We had to do hand-to-hand combat. The first time the NVA attacked and wiped out our perimeter defenses. We had the bunker phones in the FDC. We were getting calls from people begging for help. One guy was severely wounded. I had to charge across the compound and dropped down and returned fire. We kept the NVA away from the bunker. By early morning they had retreated. Several months later we were under siege for two weeks by an NVA battalion. We fought two ground battles—had to do hand-to-hand combat to kick them off the hill.

"The [U.S.] servicemen coming back became an object of hatred for the antiwar people. It was difficult. Some of my former college friends didn't want to have anything to do with me.

"You came home. You put your uniform in the closet and you tried to forget. But you can never forget what you went through. It will stay with you, and at times it will come back to haunt you."

SALUTING THEIR FALLEN COMRADES are, from left, Harris, Shyab, Burch, Funk, Jordan and Stryer.

JUST ONE MORE

A MEMORIAL to a dead American soldier in the scarred landscape of Mutter Ridge in Nui Cay Tri is left behind after the brutal fighting there in the fall of 1966. It was said that only luck might decide who would die and who would survive at Mutter Ridge. People who hadn't asked the questions before now did: What was this war? Where was the way out?